Three Years and a Half in the Army; or, History of the Second Colorados

MRS. ELLEN WILLIAMS

Three Years and a Half in the Army; or, History of the Second Colorados

Union Volunteer Cavalry at War Against Indians & Confederate Forces, 1860-65

Mrs. Ellen Williams

Three Years and a Half in the Army; or, History of the Second Colorados.
Union Volunteer Cavalry at War Against Indians & Confederate Forces,
1860-65
by Mrs. Ellen Williams

First published under the title
Three Years and a Half in the Army; or, History of the Second Colorados.

Leonaur is an imprint of Oakpast Ltd

Copyright in this form © 2011 Oakpast Ltd

ISBN: 978-0-85706-653-4 (hardcover)
ISBN: 978-0-85706-654-1 (softcover)

http://www.leonaur.com

Publisher's Notes

The opinions of the authors represent a view of events in which she was a participant related from her own perspective, as such the text is relevant as an historical document.

The views expressed in this book are not necessarily those of the publisher.

Contents

Preface	7
War is Declared	9
The Enemy Advances	13
Operations Around Santa Fe	23
Marching Orders	31
Bushwacked	49
Operations Against Prices Invasion	58
Death of Major Smith	68
The Surrender of General Marmaduke	81
The Final Pursuit of the Rebel Army	93
My Farewell to the Regiment	101
Indian Attack	111
Appendix 1	118
Appendix 2	123

Preface

In placing this work before the public the author has but one aim; that is, to give to the soldiers of Colorado a record which shall impart pleasure to themselves, their families and friends; the reading of it will take them over the same ground again, through the same hardships, showing their powers of endurance, of bravery and valour; bringing to mind no doubt much of personal knowledge which the author could not reach, hence it is missing, but she trusts they will grant she has done the best possible with the means at command, trying to make it an interesting, truthful account of brave acts and deeds, with all reverence, respect and kindness for the soldiers of Colorado whose hardships with her husband she shared.

Ellen Williams.

Chapter 1

War is Declared

In the summer of eighteen hundred and sixty, to any one taking a bird's-eye view of the different mining districts of Colorado, it bore much the appearance of a beehive.

The mountains were perforated with holes in which were at work a countless number of men. And as they moved in and out they resembled the busy insect.

The work went on day by day; to some Dame Fortune gave favours; to some disappointment. Now and then an excitement of new discoveries disturbed the regular routine of labour.

And the arrival of the mail from the States with news from home sometimes made slight changes.

Soon that event began to be one of intense interest, the papers contained accounts of trouble, and later the cry flew like wildfire, war is declared.

Then followed the sound of fife and drum. Recruiting officers were to be found in every available point, and men flocked to the standard of their country, and enlisted to aid in putting down the enemy. When this great rebellion broke out, the shock was felt, not only in the immediate locality of the outbreak, but extended all over the continent, from the Atlantic to the Pacific coast.

The echo of the first gun fired on Sumpter had scarcely died away, when the loyal men of the loyal States and Territories rose in their might, and asked to be led against the "invaders of peace and enemies of free institutions." Conspicuous among that number was the Territory of Colorado. Although but a child in years, and separated from the States by a vast sandy plain; with a population composed of all classes, representing almost every State and Government on the Globe, yet the great heart of her people throb bed with loyal pulsation, and loyal blood coursed through her every vein. When the war was forced upon her by the rebels, true to her allegiance to the Government of the United States, Colorado called the roll of loyalty and honour, and a thousand brave hearts and willing hands came up and answered to their names, exchanging "Pick and Shovel" for the "Sword and Bayonet," and marched forth to meet the rebel hordes that were over-running and desolating the fair and wealthy soil of Texas and New Mexico, and threatening even Colorado herself.

How well the work was done, may readily be ascertained by pointing to the bloody battlefields of Valverde, Pigeon's Ranch, Apache Canon, etc., where the soldiers of Colorado, assisted by a portion of the New Mexican forces under General Canby, met and signally defeated the rebels under the notorious Sibley, driving them like chaff before the wind, thus rescuing from their unhallowed grasp the fertile soil of New Mexico, and the rich gold deposits of Colorado, a prize they strongly coveted, and a project in which had they succeeded, would have blasted her prospects perhaps for years to come. For even a small force in the mountains, and well acquainted with the passes and fastnesses, could have kept at bay and bid defiance to an army ten times their superior in point of numbers, and have proved a serious obstacle for the already heavily burdened, although "not exhausted," government in crushing out the most gigantic rebellion on record.

The ranks of the Second Colorado Regiment were composed of the hardy miners, inured to toil and privation, with but little experience in the art of war, and that little confined, at first, principally to the two Independent Companies, A and B. These two companies were organized in the fall of '61, and mustered into service under Captain Ford, afterward colonel of the regiment of which these two companies became a part, and Captain Dodd, afterward lieutenant-colonel.

About the first of December, Company B, and a few days after, Company A, received marching orders to report in Fort Garland, New Mexico, there to be mustered into the service of the United States. Accordingly, after a few days of marching through the valleys and over the mountains, we reached the garrison, then in command of Major Whiting, of the regular United States army. There was but little worth recording during the march, save the fact that we passed a Mexican lying by the roadside, who had been dead several weeks, yet the body was as perfect as if but sleeping, even the eyes, which were open, were plump and full, and although wolves, panthers, wild-cats, bears, and other ferocious animals were plenty there, the body had never been touched, which to us was a source of surprise. On inquiry, we were informed the man had shot an American and in turn was shot, and our informant added, "nothing will eat a Mexican." And so it seemed.

The two companies were duly mustered in and put on duty in the garrison to await further orders. As horses could not be procured just then they took their place as infantry, doing duty in turn with the regular soldiers already stationed there.

Major Whiting, the officer in command of Fort Garland, was one of the regular army, and decidedly rigid, anything out of the old military order greatly annoyed him. As recruiting had been such a sudden event it had been impossible to procure military clothing fast enough, and so the raw recruit was easily known there by the mixture of his garments, part citizen, part soldier. Among other things, overcoats were scarce articles; expecting to get them at the fort, and fine weather when leaving Canon City did not show their necessity. One cold grey overcoat was all company A could muster. At one corner of the garrison, where a guard had to walk his beat, it was extremely cold, a draft cutting through all the time, consequently the old grey coat was called into requisition, to the infinite disgust of the major, who turned to the orderly, Pat Ford, asking him if the same man was always on guard, and received for answer, "No, be jabers, but the same coat kivers the whole company now."

THE MAJOR'S LAMENT.

'Tis there when the moon so pale and still
Is throwing its beams o'er the murmuring rill,
'Tis there when the morning sun's bright sheen
On each mountain top is seen.

'Tis there by night, 'tis there by day,
The same old coat of dusky grey,
Its patches too, I do declare,
It is the same, 'tis always there.

Wher'er I look the guard in sight
Is bearing that hideous grey old fright,
'Tis surely ominous of ill,
It sends through me a nervous thrill.

At midnight when all others rest
My mind by dreams is sore opprest,
I wake and murmur in despair
That same grey coat is always there.

I wish some pitying soul would take
That coat and burn it for my sake,
Or cast its shreds to the winds of heaven,
The act I am sure would be forgiven.

ANSWER.

That coat has proved the friend indeed,
Look kindly on our friend in need,
That same old coat, through wind and storm,
Hath many a heart kept warm.

The soldier cold, and sparsely clad,
E'en of the old grey coat was glad,
Then scorn it not, though worn and grey,
Nor throw the soldier's friend away.

Chapter 2

The Enemy Advances

Scarcely had the companies began to learn the ways of garrison life, ere reports came to the effect that the rebels were marching from Texas on to Mexico and Colorado, taking all garrisons on the route, thus supplying themselves with arms, clothing, etc., and, as many joined them, it was giving them strength and encouragement. Simultaneously came the order for Co. B to report at Santa Fe, in New Mexico, and from thence were hurried on to Fort Craig, to join the forces there under General Canby, where the enemy were daily expected. None too soon did they arrive, as a desperate encounter took place which resulted in great loss to the enemy, and some to the troops under General Canby. The rebels there met a class of men who gave them reason to be less sanguine than they had been. Company B were dauntless and brave, and with Lieutenant Dodd on the lead they presented a solid breast to the enemy, meeting the lancers as they came, each man with his bayonet unhorsed the oncoming foe.

The enemy were repulsed and badly demoralized. The Battle of Valverde, New Mexico, took place on the twenty-first of February, 1862. Company B, of the Second Colorado, made one out of five companies to support McRea's Battery, and afterward rein forced Colonel Roberts, in each place grandly performing their duty. Two men were killed and several were wounded. The battle of Valverde was a fierce and desperate fight. Much blood was shed on both sides; it left many wounded, dying and dead.

In the battle General Canby showed himself the brave, considerate commander and after it was over, as he went through the ranks of the wounded, he wept as only a comrade would who loved his fellow soldier; a truly noble man he was. Meanwhile the report of the enemy below came to Fort Garland as fast as mule dispatches could bear it, and with it orders for Company A, of the Second Colorado (of which my husband was bugler), to march as soon as possible, and report at Santa Fe, in New Mexico, for further orders.

Accordingly, on the fourth day of February, drawing ten days' rations, Company A, with Captain Ford in command, started on one of the most perilous marches of the war. The second night out we camped on the Rio Grande, or Grand River. Three wagons had been chartered to convey us to Santa Fe; to each one was attached six yoke of oxen. The first intention was to cross the San Antonie Mountains, it being the shortest road. We therefore crossed the river and proceeded. As we went on, each day was giving us more difficult roads and deeper snows and intensely cold weather. The frost was severe; it broke the king-bolt of one of the heavy freight wagons like it was a pipe-stem—a bolt of iron as large as one's wrist. That left a part of the company without beds or bedding, and in consequence we had to camp at the first spot available for water, as near to the damaged wagon as possible, to admit of its being repaired early next day.

The spot was an open plateau, at the foot of the mountains, very cold and breezy; we all suffered intensely. A pail of water brought from the stream and placed by our tent, in an hour had frozen so much you could not dip a small cup in the centre. We were all glad to eat our frozen piece and crawl under the blankets as soon as possible. Placing my children (I had two little ones) between my husband and myself, to keep them from perishing, thinking they were safe, I can assure you, I was fatigued enough to sleep soundly myself till reveille in the morning. Couriers were sent ahead to see if it was possible to get through on the route. They returned with the information that the mountains were impassable; trains were already blocked in forty feet of snow.

We had then to retrace our steps to return to the camping ground of the Rio Grande, cross over and try a more southern route through the Taos Valley. Napoleon's march across the Alps was made the theme of song and story, but it would sink into insignificance if compared with the marches of the Second Regiment of Colorado, especially of Companies A and B. Mexico was a trackless waste, alternately long narrow valleys and ranges of irregular mountains covered with a growth of pine cedar and scrub oak, which during winter are loaded down with snow.

There are no roads, but just a trail made by the *burros*, which the natives pack with their goods whenever they wish to transport them to any place.

I have seen a household packed on one of the little long-eared creatures, even women and their trunks; there was but little in sight except the ears and legs of the poor animal.

But to go back to our march. Some days we could only make about two miles. In selecting this route our guides had hopes of less snow, but it seemed as if we could scarce encounter more difficulty. Snows would fall at night covering up tents and wagons, and all track or trail was out of sight. Squads of the soldiers would march ahead to break the track, alternately changing to rest each other, while others with shovels went ahead of the teams to clear the way for the poor jaded animals, and (allowing a military term) bringing up the rear was my two children and myself; my baby boy was most of the time in the arms of one or other of the soldiers, his comrade relieving him of his gun. To ride was impossible, as that would be to freeze or to risk a roll down the mountain side, as one misstep of a poor toiling beast might have hurled the wagons down into the deep ravines, burying all out of sight in the snow.

One day of this trying march across the Ratoon Mountains, I think will never be forgotten by any of those who were there. We started up from Red River in the morning. It was extremely cold, and the mountains very steep; hopes were entertained of reaching feed and water at night for the sake of the poor cattle.

After starting out it was found impossible to proceed without doubling teams; all the oxen had to be attached to one wagon, and then it seemed scarcely to move, even with all their united efforts.

Those of the soldiers not needed to help with the wagons subsequently started to ascend the mountains, my husband with the rest, my children and myself following behind. About a mile up it became so cold, the sharp stinging wind cutting face and fingers, that my little boy began to cry, all effort to make him forget it was of no avail. We had out-walked the teams, and it became evident they would be some time reaching where we were. The soldiers proposed and prepared to carry into effect the idea of making a fire.

You may imagine what a task it was, when not a spot of bare ground could be seen. The trees being weighted down with snow. But to say, was to do with the hardy mountaineer. Overcoats were pulled off and placed on the snow under a pinon tree, and then I was requested to sit down with my children and coats were hung around us for protection, till a fire could be started. Then came the task of digging out dead wood from under the snow, but as many hands make quick work, a pile was soon raised. Next came the hunt for matches with which to start the cheering blaze. *Snap, snap, snap*, still no fire, only one match was left, all efforts had been futile, till now came the glowing spark from the last match, and soon we were sitting and some standing in the melted snow.

We heeded not the wet, the fire was so pleasant to our senses in our benumbed condition. While enjoying the fire a messenger came, telling us the teams could make but a very short distance that day. As they told us where to find a camping ground for the night, we left our cheerful fire and started on, reaching the ground designated.

Beneath the shelter of some friendly pinon trees our tents were placed as soon as the wagons reached the ground. Meals were then prepared and quickly disposed off.

The poor tired animals were driven back to Red River, our

starting point (in the morning), to be fed. Nothing was to be had on the mountain top. For one week the poor tired creatures had to be driven back each night to be fed. You may therefore judge we could not travel far in the day.

When we awoke next morning we found ourselves buried in snow, and heard the captain bawling round, "Charley, where are you?" (to my husband) who soon started a fire inside, which sent the snow rolling off the tent. Marching through the snow was again the order of the day, with the same programme as before, with slight variations, one of which was tying ropes to one side of the wagons, the men hanging with all their, might to stop them from rolling down the precipice into the ravines beneath, which were filled with snow. We were just climbing round the mountains to reach the valley on the other side, and thus it was for about twenty days, sky above and snow beneath, tramping wearily along.

Not hearing from the company, the officers in command at Santa Fe became uneasy and sent out scouts to hunt us up. On learning our whereabouts, mule teams were sent to relieve the jaded oxen, and to hurry us on to Santa Fe, where marching orders were waiting for the company, and all the troops stationed there to push on soon as possible to Fort Union. The military supplies for the territories and the arsenal were kept there, and it was deemed advisable to protect that garrison, it being the best stronghold, and the enemy were reported marching in full force for that point, as it would give them control of the whole frontier, and most of the supplies needed for a large body of troops.

With the reinforcement of teams, we soon reached Santa Fe, where all was bustle preparing to march. Our tents were speedily put up and we were soon eating the first square meal for twenty-eight days; that you may imagine, when you remember we started with only ten days' rations, and we had travelled through a country where money would have been but little benefit if we had been fortunate enough to possess it. The settlements were few and very far between, and at best not very inviting; the inhabitants were Mexicans, and mostly *peons*, guarding the herds or flocks of their masters.

Now came the most trying time for me. After getting through that far, hoping to be able to keep with or near my husband, I found orders for all women to stay in Santa Fe. Accordingly, my husband and his comrades found a room in which they placed my few earthly possessions, that consisted of bedding, clothes and food. Soldiers don't get burdened with household effects; at least, we did not. I stepped in that room not knowing how long I would have even that roof over my head. I dared not to think, what the war might bring to me. I was penniless, for we had taken no pay, although six months in the army.

I dared not to think, perhaps I might be left alone with my two little boys, a stranger there. I could not understand one word of Spanish or talk it, and perhaps in the end I might have to beg my way back to my friends. I never thought of the dark side. I only lived with the hope that all would be right; that my husband would be spared, and I be near him when he needed a wife's care. I never dreamed that the American Government might disown me or throw aside my claims as a soldier's wife. But such things have been done, and many have suffered. It has made me shudder often when I look back and think what might have been. In a few hours the troops were called into line and marched through the square and out of sight, *en route* to meet the enemy who were expected to put in an appearance any minute.

As the troops passed out of sight, I stood with my two little boys in the doorway watching them. A sense of loneliness came over me, such as I never felt before. Hundreds of miles from home and kindred, among a nation of people whose language I could not understand, and although a few Americans were in business there yet the Spanish language was all that was spoken. Scarcely had I began to realize my situation before my thoughts were carried away from the subject. On the east side of the square, the flames were bursting from a dwelling which had been used as officers' quarters, and some thoughts had been entertained of putting me there, but a kind Providence spared me from a sad accident, alone as I was.

Next came an excitement, the intensity of which I can never show on paper. In less time than it takes me to write it, came Mexican men, women and children. Lame, feeble, crippled and all ages, rushing, as you will see hungry animals, after food; one pulling here and one pulling there. The building burned to the ground; it was only *adobe*, consequently there was not much to be burned beside doors and windows.

This motley crew heeded not the fire but rushed to the empty house adjacent, which had been occupied by troops, and tore therefrom everything made of either wood, iron or glass. From the wells, the buckets, chains, rollers and even the curbs passed into their hands. Like so many famishing wolves, they tore around trying to outdo each other; jostling, crowding, scolding and cursing in Spanish as they loaded down their *burros* with the plunder. A party had been left in charge of the stores of the commissary who, it was stated, sold all he could, putting the money in a safe place, and then fearing the rebels he threw out the remainder into the square and left.

It consisted of boxes of soap, rice, candles, pickles, hominy, vinegar, dried vegetables, and all such stores as are used in the army. Such a charge as they made on the provisions was scarcely ever witnessed by mortal eye, and the scene will never leave my memory; pen fails to give a fair description. All were Mexicans but one; that was the wife of a regular soldier; she was an Irishwoman, and was dressed in a bright green dress, and thus became distinguishable among them. Methinks I see her now, first here, then there, always well loaded, and it was useless for the Mexicans to interfere. She was too brisk a soldier for the natives. In spite of my discouraging situation I could but laugh at her difficulties and disputes; they were many.

This plundering was kept up till past midnight, it began about noon, a clear bright moon helping them to see their way, and their activity did not cease. In the stable-yard or corral was a large stack of hay and a great deal of firewood; after clearing all the empty houses they attacked it. I sat in the window watching the motley crew, till I fell asleep from sheer exhaustion. When daylight appeared they were still at their work, and it continued as long as there was a house to search. In fact the business men began to fear lest they would next attack their stores, so ferocious did they appear; and it did seem as if there was cause to fear; it did not look safe till in a day or two a scare was put on them by two rebels, who had been arrested subsequently in Santa Fe as spies, but were given their freedom after the troops were concentrated at Fort Union.

They returned to Santa Fe; on seeing them the Mexicans sent a cry ringing on the air "*Tehanna, Tehanna*," which meant "Texan," of whom they stood in great fear, the men seeing, which I think helped the excitement. The Mexicans were afraid to occupy their separate beds, and could be seen dragging their beds and bedding into as few rooms as they could possibly inhabit. The two men, desiring to show a little authority, came around to where I was living, and one desired me to make preparation to move as soon as I could. Seeing I was feeling quite sick, I suppose that caused them to be civil. I promised to move as soon as I could get a house to live in, and he passed on a few doors further, where lived my friend of the green dress, and I soon saw from the gestures of the two there was an altercation; and as he backed out she stepped up.

At last he exclaimed: "If you don't move out I will burn the house over your head." She stepped up to him, and slapping one hand in the palm of the other, she said in anything but polite language, "Burn away, burn away, I can put as many sticks on the fire as you can." I think he took her word for that; at least that was the last we heard of them.

I left the house very soon. The wife of a Mexican soldier had vacated hers from fear, and told me if I dared to live in it I could. I moved, only too glad to get where I would be free from annoyance. The Government buildings and property was the first hunted up by straggling rebels, and we were left to their tender mercies. A part of the rebel army was then making its way up to Santa Fe, when they reached Albuquerque, they gave eight of our men their liberty. They had taken them prisoners at Valverde. Truth to tell they had great need of provisions, and so it was a policy to let them go. Major Garrison and some privates of the regular army, and one or two of Company B of the Second Colorado were the prisoners. They entered the city, weary, worn and footsore, intending to proceed to join their respective commands, but advised by Mrs. General Canby they stayed a few hours taking the rest they dearly needed.

Rumours were then flying round that the rebels were then marching on to Santa Fe in great numbers sweeping the country before them, and, it seemed to us, there was truth in the report, for in a few hours stragglers began to arrive, and began to take all they could lay hands on from the soldiers' wives. Our husbands had procured for us all the provisions they could, as we were entirely without, and we could form no idea of when we could get more, and therefore had to husband our stores with great care. As soon as I heard of their plundering, my little boy and myself dug a long shaped hole in the ground at the back of the house, there we placed our sack of flour and other stores, covering them up carefully and scattered ashes and dry dirt over the place to hide the fresh digging.

About the time we had finished we learned that the officer in command was Captain Battles, with whom our captain's wife was acquainted, and at her request he put a stop to such doings. So our scare then was at an end, as far as ourselves were concerned, but it only gave place to a greater anxiety each moment. We were listening for the boom of cannons, we feared the worst, for our troops were so few in number, and rumour told of the thousands who were marching on from Texas sweeping all before them.

At this critical moment, the heart of a true good woman, showed itself. Mrs. Canby, wife of the poor murdered general who lost his life in the Modoc Nation, urged all loyal women to help make preparation for such wounded as might need care, herself setting the example, by having beds filled, hospital rooms set in order, lint, soups and everything she could think of, prepared for the comfort and aid of the suffering. When expostulated with for so doing, as rebel wounded might be the ones, her answer was that of a pure loving Christian woman. It was this, "No matter whether friend or foe, our wounded enemy must be cared for and their lives saved if it is possible, they are sons of some dear mother." Her total disregard of self and watchful care of the suffering men, tending with her own hand at every place where she saw most need of woman's care, won for her the love of friend and foe alike.

Chapter 3

Operations Around Santa Fe

While this was going on, the roar of cannon was heard. The din of war reverberated through the surrounding country, and, only too soon, wounded men were brought to the city, maimed, suffering and dying. They were promptly attended to, although they were from the Confederate lines. Subsequently an engagement had taken place. The Confederate forces had entrenched and fortified themselves, and totally unexpected our forces found themselves obliged to stand on the defensive. The Texans had taken a stand, which for a time seemed to give them the advantage in position and certainly they had it in point of numbers. So sure were they of success, that they had placed their supply train containing provisions, arms, ammunition, clothes and so forth, for their army, in a canon in their rear with a guard of only two hundred men in charge.

This circumstance gave our men great aid, as in my further history I shall show. A little strategy placed it in their hands. While part of our troops were coping with the enemy, braving to all appearance certain death, a small handful of men under Major Chivington, led by a scout, and marching round the mountain went to where their supply train was placed, which they attacked. Some were taken prisoners, some fled panic-stricken, and in less time than it takes me to tell it, a roar as if the mountains were rent in twain arose on the air; they had fired the train, and in a few seconds nothing but the smoke and ashes was left of that which was to sustain the large Confederate force then in the territory and at that time engaged in a battle with our forces at Apache Canon. While this small band succeeded in effectually crippling the enemy, their comrades were engaged in one of the most brilliant battles of the war. We find the official records fail to give the credit to the soldiers of Colorado. Yet their success was mainly due to them.

Their coolness and bravery was without a parallel. Sergeant Jones of Company A, who helped to man one of the batteries, when the shot and shell was flying around him like hail, hurling trees and rocks and making the mountains tremble, turned to his comrades, so deliberately, and said: "Boys they like grape, let's give 'em a little more."

I think the unfairness of official record was mainly due to the fact that it was from the regular officers' mostly, and they had not much kind feeling for the volunteers. I can here give the part taken by Colonel Slough of the first regiment of Colorado, he was in command of the division composed of the following troops: his own regiment, the First Regiment of Colorado, Captain Ford's Independent Company of Volunteers, afterwards A of the Second Regiment of Colorado, Captain Lewis' Battalion of Fifth Infantry, Captain Ritter's Battery, Lieutenant Clafflin's Battery and four small howitzers. The movement commenced from Fort Union, Saturday, the twenty-second of March, and the command encamped at Vernal Springs, forty-five miles from Union, on Tuesday, the twenty-fifth instant.

On Wednesday, the twenty-sixth, a command of two hundred cavalry and one hundred and eighty infantry, under Major Chivington of the First Regiment of Colorado, was advanced toward Santa Fe, with a view of capturing or defeating a force of the enemy reported to be stationed there. The enemy in force was engaged near Johnston's Ranch, Apache Canon, about fifteen miles from Santa Fe. The result was victorious to our forces. The enemy was defeated with some twenty or twenty-five killed, more wounded, and about seventy taken prisoners. Our loss was small. Three men killed in the fight, two died from wounds and some eight others wounded. Captain Cook of the

Colorado Volunteers was very badly wounded, but recovered after a long sickness.

Major Chivington's command, Company A, under command of Captain Ford, formed a part of the same, and took position on the Pecas, at Kaslowski's Ranch, twenty-seven miles from Santa Fe. About noon on the twenty-seventh, Colonel Slough left Camp Paul, at Bernal Springs, and about two o'clock next morning posted his entire force at Kaslowski's. On the twenty-eight, a movement was made upon the enemy in columns, with a view of reconnoitring his position at Johnston's Ranch. For this purpose the infantry force of regulars and volunteers, under Major Chivington, was directed to move off on the Galisteo road, attain the principal height upon the side of Apache Canon and occupy them.

While the main body, under Colonel Slough, moved directly into the canon. It was known that the enemy had been strongly reinforced. At nine o'clock in the morning our troops left their encampment and at thirty minutes past ten arrived at Pigeon's Ranch, five miles distant, and please bear in mind, it was a rocky, mountainous country through which they had to pass, it was almost impossible to set a sure foot on the loose pebbles. The command, under Major Chivington, had flanked off at a point about two miles beyond Kaslowski's.

When Colonel Slough's command reached Pigeon's, he directed Captain Chaplin, Seventh Infantry, adjutant-general, to proceed forward with the cavalry and reconnoitre the position of the enemy. He had proceeded about three hundred yards when our pickets were driven in, and the enemy opened a fire of grape and shell from a battery carefully placed in position upon the hill side. The batteries were brought forward and the infantry thrown out upon the flanks. The cavalry, with an addition of infantry, supported the batteries and the firing became general. The battle continued over five hours. The fighting was all done in thick covers of cedars, and having met the enemy where they were not expected the action was defensive from beginning to end.

The capturing and destroying of the wagon train and supplies by Major Chivington's command was a most serious disaster to the enemy. About five p. m. a flag of truce came from the enemy, and measures were taken by both forces to gather up and bury their dead and to care for the wounded. All who were able to be moved were brought to Santa Fe, and Rebel as well as Union men shared alike the kindness and care of the doctors and citizens. Mrs. General Canby personally seeing that none should suffer for care. The wounded who could not be brought to the city were her special charge; her carriage could be seen every day on the road, bearing her or something her thoughtful care had provided for the sick and suffering.

As there was positive orders for Fort Union to be protected at all hazards, Colonel Slough with his entire command fell back to that point. The Confederate forces came on to Santa Fe, where their sick and wounded lay. From privations and hardships, marching through a climate much colder than their own, disease set in and pneumonia gave the grave nearly as many as the fight. Day by day I saw the hospital wagon, with its silent load, wending its way along the mountain side, and on that lonely plateau would be laid side by side all that was left of the once healthy, robust young men who but a few weeks before left the sunny soil of Texas, leaving their beloved ones behind, never to return. A small wooden tablet marks their resting place; their names today, I expect, are faded out and they are numbered with the unknown. Finding, I suppose, nothing could be gained by holding Santa Fe, the whole Confederate force who were able to travel evacuated the city, leaving their dying to the merciful. They abandoned their sick and dying everywhere.

The Confederate forces were reported to be concentrating at or near Albuquerque, accordingly General Canby, of whose command Company B of the Second then was a part, ordered Colonel Paul, who was in command of the division at Union, to make a junction with him at the above named point, to intercept or rout the entire force of the enemy. On the evening of the thirteenth of April, a junction was formed and the whole united command was marched, during the day and night of the fourteenth, to Peralto, thirty-six miles distant, arriving there before the Confederate force had any suspicion of the movement. In this command Companies A and B of the Second Colorado were again together.

On the morning of the fifteenth, a mountain howitzer and a train seven wagons loaded with supplies, and escorted by a lieutenant and thirty men, were captured. Six of the Confederates were killed in the conflict, three wounded and twenty-two captured. To cover this movement, Colonel Paul with his column had been detached, and after completing it, he received permission to clear the *basque* in front of Peralto of the enemies force that then occupied it. After some sharp skirmishing, in which our loss was one killed and three wounded, this work was handsomely executed, and the *basque* in front and rear of the town occupied by our troops.

The point occupied by the Confederate troops was known to be the strongest, except Fort Union, in New Mexico, and as nearly all the men had been twenty-four, and many of them thirty-six hours, without food, no general attack was designed until after the approaches to the place had been thoroughly reconnoitred and the troops allowed time to obtain food and rest. This reconnoisance was made on the afternoon of the same day, the points and direction of attack selected, and the camp of the command advanced to a point nearer the town where the trains could be guarded by a smaller number of men. During the night the enemy abandoned his position and crossed to the right bank of the Rio Grande del Norte, leaving his sick and wounded behind him without attendance, without medicine and almost without food.

After detaching the staff-officers attached to the department headquarters, to make arrangements for future operations and the train that could be spared for supplies, the pursuit was continued down the left bank of the river (the shortest route) with the intention of crossing at La Foya, Palvastera, Sabina or Fort Craig, if the enemy should not be overtaken sooner. On the night of that day our camp was five miles in his rear. On the sixteenth we had nearly overtaken the rear of his column, and the march was continued during the remainder of the day in sight and almost within cannon range, but on opposite sides of the river. All night our camps were directly opposite, but during the night he abandoned a large portion of his train, thirty-eight wagons and the supplies they contained, and fled into the mountains.

After making arrangements for securing the property abandoned by the enemy, the march was continued to Balvedera. At this place the command was halted for a day, in order to be assured of the position and movements of the enemy, and to secure the safety of a supply train in our rear. These objects having been accomplished, the march was resumed and continued till the command reached Fort Craig on the afternoon of the twenty-second of April.

Companies A and B of the Second Colorado were ordered into the Fort, and the First Regiment of Colorado camped on the sands preparatory to being returned to Colorado. The two first named companies stayed at Fort Craig doing such duty as was from time to time assigned them, hoping for a release as it was one of the most disagreeable places in which to stay; tarantula, centipedes and tail-toads were frequent bed-fellows; the provisions were of the poorest quality, both bread and meat wormy, and the water was as thick as porridge. At last the paymaster made his appearance for the first time since enlistment, which was very nearly a year.

Our troops had but little encouragement to fight; badly clothed, badly fed, and so many months without a cent of money, but as it was unavoidable they took it philosophically and made the best of it when it came. A short time after this event, about the last of August or beginning of September, Companies A and B of the Second Colorado, with Lieutenant-Colonel Dodd in command, were ordered to report at Santa Fe, and they were very glad of the change.

A laughable incident occurred on this march. It being extremely warm it was deemed expedient, as they had a sandy desert to cross, to make that march early in the morning while cool. The bugler accordingly had orders to sound reveille as soon as the morning star appeared. He rolled up in his blankets, took a good snore or two, waking up he saw the bright star sailing along. He sounded the call, the camp was aroused, and after a little preparation the command was in motion, In vain they looked for day. Someone found out at last it was the "evening star," instead of the morning. All then declared the bugler had taken his canteen for a telescope, looking through it instead of the latter.

After a tedious march across the hot sand the command reached Santa Fe, finding it occupied by Union troops and all going on as if nothing had disturbed the peace of the country, the only evidence left was the destruction which General Canby was endeavouring to obliterate as speedily as possible, repairing all the damage caused by pillage and fire. When the Union forces evacuated the city they cut down the flag-pole, intending the rebels should never have the chance of raising their flag on it.

When our troops returned to Santa Fe, about the first order given was to make a pole to replace the one cut down and men were detailed for the purpose. My husband was one of the number and, on the fourth of July, assisted in raising the flag of the free once more in the City of Santa Fe.

It is up and it floats,
On the pure morning air,
It's stripes are uninjured,
It's stars are all there;
And long may it float, o'er the land and the sea,
Our own glorious emblem, the flag of the free.

It is up, and the sunshine,
Hath gilded the staff,
The mountains we fancy
They seem as to laugh,

May the echo go forth, o'er the land and the sea,
Our flag is afloat, 'tis the flag of the free,
See the traitors succumb,
In their rebel disgrace;
When they find our fair emblem,
Hath taken its place,
Owning that as they vanish, o'er the land and the sea,
Our flag must float ever, the flag of the free.

It is up, and its breast
Is to heaven laid bare,
Our God he hath seen it,
And blesseth it there;
It waves, aye how grandly, o'er the land and the sea,
Our flag is acknowledged, the flag of the free.

'Neath its folds our forefathers
Have bled and have died,
Victory and honour
Is to it allied;
As it spreads in its grandeur, o'er the land and the sea,
Our emblem of glory, the flag of the free.

It is up, may the heavens
Turn black with despair,
Ere 'tis torn from its homestead
And other placed there.
May the darkness of Erebus, wrap earth and the sea,
Ere they tear from its standard, the flag of the free.

Mrs. Williams.

Chapter 4

Marching Orders

It was a beautiful and impressive sight; the morning sun gilding the mountain-tops with its mellow light and reflecting its golden hues on all around us. General Canby with the officers of his staff, with bared heads; the chaplain's prayer of thankfulness; the general standing with his hand upon the pole, his fine form and noble physique; around him the officers and the soldiers under arms, ready to salute; the mountains in the background; in front, the citizens; altogether gave a picture worthy the pencil of an artist. Grandly sublime, more especially so when taking into consideration the place and general condition of the country, scarcely a step above barbarism.

The two companies, A and B, were assigned to garrison duty, a regular officer who was in command there appeared to take eminent delight in giving them duties to perform, which would lessen them as men; for instance, to clear away the slop and garbage which accumulated around the officers' quarters, and sweep the dirt from their doors. Now our volunteers did not enlist for such work, but knowing at the same time that a good soldier obeys orders, it was done, and with the labour no doubt some profanity was mixed, as soldiers under aggravating circumstances are not proof against temptation to err. Time soon became irksome to them, they had no penchant for staying around garrisons, it was active service they wanted, and when reports came that the Texans intended to try another attack on the territory, coming up by way of Red River, it gave them a hope that again they would have a show to test the mettle of the enemy.

About the time the first snow fell, Company B was ordered to report at Fort Union. On their arrival they were put on duty in the garrison where active work was going on throwing up trenches. Very shortly after, Company A was also ordered to report at the same place, and on arriving there the duty was assigned them of cutting timber for the trenches to facilitate the matter. We camped about five miles from the fort in a place called Coyote Canon, a narrow defile between the mountains, where we were surrounded with timber.

The work went actively forward for a few weeks, every means to find out the movements of the enemy, their strength and intention were made. After making a feint as if to enter the territory again they all at once disappeared, and it became evident they had abandoned the idea and instead were moving toward the Arkansas, or Indian Nation. All sign of trouble in Mexico was at an end, and the duties of the garrison was all there was to perform, except an occasional scout after prowling redskins.

About the early part of January, orders came for Companies A and B of the Second Colorado to report at Fort Lyon, accordingly the two companies left Fort Union under Captain Hall's command. I think there was but a very few regretted leaving Mexico, yet it was again mid winter. Our route this time was a more pleasant one. We did not have to encounter on this trip such inclement weather, although sometimes cold, wet and snowy, it was nothing in comparison to our other marches; it was one of pleasure, the sick outdoor patients I cared for improved every day; it was a quiet march with only the fun of camping out thrown in.

We reached Fort Lyon in the Spring of 1863, and met there a hearty welcome from the soldiers of Colorado already stationed there. As some companies of the First Regiment of Colorado were in Fort Lyon on the arrival of our two companies, A and B, the former were sent to Denver preparatory to being ordered to the States. During the time we were in Mexico, recruiting had been actively going on in Colorado and other companies had been organized, thus completing the Second Regiment of Colorado, who were then for the first time all together. They were physically as fine a regiment as ever answered the call of the roll, their bravery was such that they were held in awe by the Confederate forces. They never failed to strike terror to their ranks. Their presence had always proved a signal of defeat.

We had been in Fort Lyon but a short time before it seemed evident there would be an uprising among the Indians, and the excitement kept the regiment a great deal of the time in the saddle, scouting here and there. Some fears were entertained of their attacking the garrisons; it was evidently their intention to take advantage if the country was clear of troops. During the Spring, orders came from the department to the effect that the Second Regiment was ordered into the field to march forthwith to the States, under command of Lieutenant-Colonel Dodd.

Accordingly, all men fit for duty were duly put under marching orders. Company F was left at Fort Lyon. All men on sick report were attached to that company, my husband among the number, at that time under treatment for rheumatism. The rest of the regiment started for the States. The weather was pretty fair at first, but was very wet, cold and disagreeable before they got to the States. The regiment up to this time had not been supplied with horses, so those who were without confiscated ponies on the road, in some cases one serving two masters.

On reaching the railroad, from which point they were to be shipped to St. Louis, they had a difficulty in getting proper conveyance, the rail road company wanting to ship them like cattle; but they refused to be carried up in that manner. Finding they would not put up with such indignity, they furnished them passenger cars, and they went on their way rejoicing, reaching St. Louis in the morning, but by some mismanagement were left at the depot till noon, when they were marched to Benton Barracks and there supplied with horses, and from thence were ordered to Maravia.

Colonel Dodd was ordered to take Companies A and B, with two pieces of artillery, to escort a provision train from Fort

Scott to Fort Smith, Arkansas. When within ten miles of Fort Smith the enemy unexpectedly attacked them in a ravine of heavy brush. A desperate encounter ensued which lasted about three hours. Of the rebels, there was two to one. Fortunately our troops had no loss, but the enemy's was about twenty killed and wounded.

On this trip, seeing plenty of pigs in the woods, some of the boys concluded to try their guns on them for the sake of fresh pork, and they found them to be a great curiosity, having cloven feet or whole hoofs like a horse. The regiment was kept in the field all the Summer and Fall. Many hard marches and desperate encounters they met on their way down to Port Gibson, where they met again some of the same regiments they encountered in Mexico. There was much hard fighting, marching and counter-marching; the enemy losing heavily, with some loss to our own, who were finally ordered up to St. Louis. Company K stayed at Fort Lyon till the month of November; then Companies F, G and H of the Third Regiment, in obedience to general order, concentrated with Company K of the Second at Fort Lyon and received orders to march for the States.

Accordingly, on the twentieth day of November, 1863, with Major Pritchard in command, we started at noon and made about twelve miles. It was a fine afternoon, but toward night a cool breeze arose, bringing with it a snow storm, which was so severe that for nine days we were obliged to stay there. The wagons were almost out of sight, and the mules had to be driven back to Fort Lyon for feed. This was but a commencement of a series of storms; for two months we saw nothing but the most inclement weather; the snow came so suddenly and so severely that it found us all unprepared—no wood, and almost an impossibility to get any, and but few stoves.

The animals suffered equally with ourselves; but the government mules generally learn a thing or two, and we had some of that educated class with us. Seeing no show for fodder, in the night they went to the supply wagon of Company K and eat up the rations; appropriating flour, bread, bacon, hominy, rice, etc., for hay and corn. That made another requisition on the commissary a necessity, and men were therefore detailed to return to the fort for stoves, food and such things as were needed for the trip.

Each day we were hoping for a change in the weather. The morning would sometimes brighten up, but a few hours brought the cold wind and drifting snow. On the morning of the twenty-fifth it was cheerful and bright, but night again brought with it a most severe and terrible storm of snow. During the time we laid snow bound in this camp—called by the men, "Camp Snow Bank"—the stage for the States, from Fort Lyon, tried to make its way down to Fort Larnard, the driver was so badly frozen he laid for many months hovering between life and death, and recovered at last to be a hopeless cripple. Many of our men were frostbitten and suffered intensely from the biting cold winds.

After we started, each day was almost a repetition of the other. Few marches on record equal this one in severity, suffering and exposure. Not a friendly tree to screen us from the storm, the open, bleak plains before and behind us, and for miles nothing to burn but weeds; every available piece of wood was used up. Two freighters who had taken up apples, butter, eggs, etc., to the Fort followed the command down. Their teams were six yoke of oxen, with very heavy freight wagons. Their cattle all perished but one yoke; the wood work of the wagons they used, as long as they could avail themselves of a splinter, and no doubt they thought themselves very fortunate in getting through alive to the Missouri River.

Each day as it advanced brought with it the same repetition of snow and bad weather. Many incidents occurred which helped to change the monotony of marching day by day through the storm, some laughable and others rather of the irritable order. One man who loved the ardent, desiring to warm the inner man, and intending to do so at the expense of the sick, went slyly to the hospital ambulance and taking therefrom a half-pint bottle of burning fluid (in mistake for whiskey) drank it down, and the result was a very sick man. He was placed in the ambulance, the end gate turned down that his head could reach over. As he lay there vomiting he was the picture of forlorn misery, many jokes were passed at his expense. Lieutenant Gooding, created a laugh by saying: "Boys, don't let the fluid waste, we will put a wick in his mouth tonight and use him for a lamp."

One night, a very hard wind was blowing, with snow and hail cutting through the air, the Sibley tents were twisting and screaming as if in torture, when all at once a gust stronger than the rest tore out the guides of one next to ours; it was occupied by our good-natured professor, Tom Willey, his wife and baby; the wind carried the fire from the stove into the bed, and while she was struggling to keep the fire from consuming the bed, he was pulling at the ropes calling for help; and the hail stinging his bare limbs, made him dance to a tune he had never learned to play on his violin, an instrument he was very fond of.

On the eighteenth of December, a young buffalo ran into camp and paid for its temerity with its life. Its carcass was a great luxury and much enjoyed by us all; a portion was handed over to me. I was always remembered if there was anything to share. The next day was extremely cold with very rough wind; but, as if by way of compensation, we found the best camping ground it had been our fortune to obtain. It was called Walnut Creek. There was plenty of wood, water and good shelter. A stage-station was there which seemed to bid us hope that we would, after a while, find more dwellings.

On the following day we passed another, and as we were now on the Smoky Hill route, ranches became more frequent and from them we were able to get feed for the animals, which began to show the evidence of hard suffering on the march; and the men began to feel as if it was home coming, for here were small porkers running around and it was quite a frolic to the boys to give them chase as they scampered away through the bush. Here was fresh pork, sausage, and pies and cakes for sale, which after such a march was a delight to our vision.

Here Major Pritchard gave orders for a general cleaning up, ever soldier thenceforth making quite a different appearance.

The next morning ushered in the twenty-second day of the month; we started, passing through the town of Salina, in Kansas, and camped five miles beyond in a belt of timber, which seemed alive with chickens, quail and turkeys, and at a ranch across the river were four tame buffalos, used on the place to haul logs, etc. Reports here reached us of the northern Sioux Indians being on the war-path and committing depredations, but we saw none of them.

We started again when the bugle sounded the forward, crossed the Solomon Ferry, and here a mule fell on a broken bridge, one leg slipping through a hole in the plank, but it was helped out with but little damage. At our next camping place some went to a house nearby and partook of a hotel dinner. It cost twenty-five cents; that was great extravagance for a poor soldier after living in the snow on hard tack and beans so long. It was a luxury to set down on a chair in a house even.

Christmas morning came to us in a pouring rain, the mud knee deep; we passed through Junction City, a nice little town, and on to Fort Riley. Here we went into quarters, which was a great treat after such a hard trip.

We saw but little here to remind us we were in the States, only one company and a small guard set who seemed mostly beardless boys.

There was far more discipline in Colorado, but the garrison did one good to look at; a soldier could but be clean here. The buildings were finished off in a first-class style. Standing as it does above the Republican River, which runs through a belt of timber, winding round the garrison, it makes a picturesque spot. Even the stables, corn-cribs, pastures and yards are finished off in a neat and complete manner, giving it a tasty appearance. We stayed there to rest for a few days and the weather moderated some. The first day out from Fort Riley was fine. We crossed the Manhattan Bridge and camped on the bottom. It was an extremely wet camping ground, we had to cut a brush pile to place our beds on; the ground was so wet and soft the tent pins were pushed in by hand.

The weather changed so suddenly in the night that next morning they had to be chopped out with an axe. We crossed the Kansas River on the ice and passed through Topeka, then but a small town. We would try to obtain shelter some nights in some of the many houses we passed, but in only two or three cases succeeded. No one appeared to pity us poor women and children out in that inclement weather. Day by day it grew colder, and the Doctor bade us stop and take possession of an empty log cabin by the roadside and there stay till the weather moderated if it took us all winter. That was the order of Doctor Vance as he rode off to catch up with the command.

As a good soldier obeys orders we halted, and driving the teams round to the shelter of the cabin unhitched, and some of the boys building a fire in the wide fireplace we prepared the supper, and such a one as it was I shall never forget. The beef, of which we had a fair supply, and potatoes, were so frozen that it was impossible to make any impression on them with a knife. To peel the latter was impossible; to throw them away would never do, for we had been so long without potatoes—they were the gift of a good Union man on our route. One of the men therefore suggested that we hash up together both beef and potatoes. Accordingly he took an axe and laying both on a clean board he minced all up fine together, and if there was a little soil mixed in, I must say, I never relished a meal half as well before or since.

We piled the bags on high and wide, but Mrs. Willey and myself could do but little else than shiver, although the warmest place was given us. It was I think the coldest night I ever witnessed. The poor mules although sheltered by the two wagons and house seemed to be almost perishing on their feet, as they stamped and kicked in the cold night air. Here we passed from 1863 to 1864.

The next morning we started to catch up with the command. It was very bright, but cold and frosty during the day. Seeing a pedestrian on the road our men inquired if he had seen the command pass by. His answer was, "Yaw, yaw; they gone, you take this road, 'tis the shortest; you turn dis way, to de left (with a motion of the hand), and you will cross a leetle pridge over the creek, keep to the left, you will get to Cedar Creek where they will camp tonight." We did so, and, as he said, made camp in good season.

Mr. McDougal and family and a Mr. Murphy should have especial mention, for they were extremely kind and thoughtful. They sent down straw to the camp for the men to sleep on, as the ground was covered with snow, and, in addition, they gave them fresh pork and potatoes, which was one of the greatest treats possible, also inviting the families to go to their houses and partake of their hospitality. Their kindness I shall never forget. The march was telling heavily upon my health, and the fatigue of setting tent, packing and unpacking, was for once omitted much to my comfort. I was thoroughly interviewed by their pleasing daughters, from whom their mother had to beg me off to get a little rest.

We pursued our way next day. It was hard to see the men footsore, frostbitten and weary. After a few more days of travel we reached Kansas City. Snow still covered the ground. The soldiers camped in it for a few days, when they were ordered to quarters to report for duty and await the arrival of the rest of the regiment, then on their way up from St. Louis. Mr. Willey and my husband rented two rooms in the outskirt of the town, so as to be handy to do their duty as buglers.

While Major Pritchard's command was crossing the plains to the States, the rest of the Second Colorado Regiment, then doing duty down in the Arkansas Nation, received orders to march and report at Kansas City, preparatory to consolidation. The Second had in its many battles and skirmishes lost many of its brave boys, and as the Third Regiment had never been full an order was issued from headquarters, Department of Missouri, announcing the organization of the Second Colorado Cavalry, as formed by the consolidation of the Second and Third Regiments, as directed in Special Order Number 278, Headquarters Department of Missouri.

When organized, its officers were as follows: James H. Ford, colonel; Theodore H. Dodd, lieutenant-colonel; Samuel S. Curtis, first major, J. Nelson Smith, second major; Jesse L. Pritchard, third assistant surgeon; D. M. Vance, assistant surgeon; Robert S. Roe, adjutant; J. S. Cook, quartermaster (who afterward resigned, and Guy C. Manville was promoted to the position); James Burrell, commissary; L. Hamilton, chaplain. Companies K of the Second and F, G and H of the Third Infantry, were broken up and the men assigned to the other companies composing the regiment, consisting of twelve companies and numbering in .all over one thousand, one hundred men.

The consolidation having been completed, the regiment was mounted on horses furnished by the government, or rather by government contractors, and said by many to be the finest lot of horses in the department, which opinion could be fully admitted on comparison with that of other regiments. A considerable number were, however, entirely unfit for service, as experience proved; breaking down with the least exertion, proving utterly incapable of performing the duty required of cavalry horses. The regiment was armed with the government sabre, Star's carbine, an arm capable of throwing a ball with great force and precision when properly adjusted, but of uncertain fire, a very important defect, when the life of a brave man was depending; also Star's revolver, a good pistol, with one serious objection, the revolving apparatus was liable get to out of order after a few discharges. It seemed strange, with such imperfect arms, so few accidents should happen, only one or two being the result therefrom.

On the sixteenth of January, the regiment was placed on the cars and started for Kansas City, Missouri, arriving at Dresden (at that time the terminus of the Pacific Railroad and distant from St. Louis about two hundred miles) the next day. The night was extremely cold, and the men, a large number of them, were placed in the cars without stoves or fire, and experienced great difficulty in keeping from freezing, being confined to the limits of the crowded cars with but little room for exercise. The horses were crowded into as small a space as possible in the open cars for sure conveyance, but a large number were severely "corked," caused by the sudden starting and stopping of the train.

On arriving at Dresden the regiment went into Camp Smith, where it remained, with the exception of the battalion that proceeded to Kansas City, until about the fifteenth of February, when it again took up the line of march, and passing through Warrensburgh on the sixteenth, arrived at Kansas City about the twentieth of February, 1864.

In passing through the counties of Jackson and Cass, the country was found to be overrun with marauders. These marauders, or *banditti*, became so numerous and bold in their nefarious trans actions, and such difficulty was experienced in apprehending and punishing the guilty, that it was deemed necessary, in order to insure justice to all parties, to cause the immediate abandonment by the inhabitants of these counties. About the twenty-third of September, 1863, the order was issued by General Ewing, giving them fifteen days to leave the counties, which was speedily obeyed by the inhabitants. Troops were stationed in the different parts of the sub-district, and the country overran; houses burned to the ground, causing the country once so fertile to resemble a wilderness, with homes deserted, fields of ground abandoned by the faithful plough. It looked sad, but it left no sustenance for the bush whackers, and but few places of shelter.

Of that few they were ever ready to take advantage, hiding behind there friendly walls and at every opportunity shooting at our troops who had occasion to go near or past; it was their favourite pastime and mode of warfare, to take our troops unaware, never in any instance meeting them bravely face to face. On the fourteenth of January, 1864, General Brown, who was at that time in command of the district of Central Missouri, issued an order from headquarters, allowing all loyally disposed citizens, who had been driven from their homes, to return on conditions, *viz.*: that they should be ever ready to assist the government in its endeavours to put down the rebellion, and protect themselves and their homes from all enemies. The same general order assigned Colonel James H. Ford, Second Colorado Cavalry, to the command of the fourth sub-district, district of Missouri, headquarters at Kansas City, Missouri.

Colonel Ford assumed command on the eighteenth day of February, and appointed Lieutenant E. L. Berthoud, then of Company E, acting assistant adjutant-general, and Captain J. C. W. Hall, of Company B, assistant provost-marshal.

On assuming command, Colonel Ford proceeded to distribute his forces throughout the sub-district, in such a manner as would be best calculated to conduct the campaign against the squads of bushwhackers, and at the same time be able to concentrate his forces with little delay on the appearance of a superior force of the enemy. Among the stations announced were the following: Kansas City, Independence, eight miles east, West Point, three miles south, Hickmann's Mills, sixteen miles south, Pleasant Hill, thirty-five miles south-east, and Harrisonville, about forty-five miles south from Kansas City. At this time the bushwhackers were comparatively quiet, confining their efforts to an occasional midnight assassination or robbery, evidently deferring operations on a large scale until the leaves came out on the trees to afford them protection in their fiendish work.

Nevertheless, the troops at the different stations were not idle, but were actively engaged in scouring the country and becoming acquainted with its geographical position, the roads and byways, learning each nook and corner as well as the inhabitants, who consisted chiefly of "widows" (?) whose husbands had gone to the war and who were strictly loyal to the government of the southern confederacy! So much diligence was exercised by the troops, that by the first of June there was scarcely a locality, road or bypath through the country, including the famous Sni Hills, with which they were not thoroughly familiar; a very important feature in hunting bushwhackers.

Many were the ruses and schemes employed by our soldiers to discover the haunts of these brigands. After dashing up to and surrounding houses at dead of night when the male inmates, who were supposed to be in the brush, would be likely to visit their homes, and not unfrequently repeating their visit the same night in order to entrap anyone who had watched their movements and supposed them far away. It was a dangerous, as well as unpleasant duty to perform, not knowing what moment a leaden message of death would be sent crashing through the brain from the hands of an unseen foe, who lay in ambush waiting for the troops to pass and who almost universally possessed the advantage of having the first fire (which was generally their last), their cowardly dispositions not allowing them to dare risk an open conflict, unless they possessed superior advantages in the strength of their forces.

Little was accomplished by either party until about the first of May, after the trees and brush were densely covered with leaves sufficient to screen the *banditti* in their nefarious transactions, and protect them from the scrutinizing search of the troops, who were almost constantly hunting for them using every means in their power to catch, destroy and drive from the country the villainous scoundrels.

Sergeant P. F. Russell, of Company I, with twenty men, had been stationed at Dayton, a small town on Grand River in Cass County, to watch the crossing. On the morning of the twenty-seventh of April, a party of men clothed in Federal uniform were seen passing near the station, and Russell supposing them to be some of our own men rode out to halt them. As they were passing over a point of rising ground two of the party were seen to fall in the rear apparently awaiting for Russell to come up, when they all disappeared over the brow of the hill. Mistrusting some foul play a reconnoisance was made, but nothing could be seen of the party; two days afterward the body of Russell was found about eight miles from Dayton, on the prairie pierced through the head with a ball and his watch and money taken. He evidently did not discover his fatal mistake until arriving in their midst, and was surrounded and hurried away utterly unable to offer any resistance. The band was a part of Quantrell's or Todd's gang.

About the same time, Privates Stone and Johnson of the same company, while carrying dispatches from Harrisonville to Johnstown, were fired upon by a party of bushwhackers on Grand

River and driven back across the stream. They succeeded in making their escape, after running many narrow chances for life, and reached Johnstown three days afterward. A party of four or five widows (?) living in the eastern part of Jackson County, and whose husbands were known to be in the brush, were arrested about the twentieth of May, and sent to Kansas City in charge of Sergeant Freeman and seven men. The escort returning the next day were ambushed by a party of bushwhackers, twenty-five or thirty in number, near the crossing of the Little Blue on the Independence and Lone Jack road.

One of the boys by the name of Vogt was shot twice through the head and fell dead from his horse; another by the name of Sowell, was severely wounded and fell from his horse, but partially recovering succeeded in getting remounted behind Sergeant Freeman, who exhibited great courage and presence of mind during the affray, but soon afterward Sowell received another shot in the head which felled him the second time; but, surprising to relate, succeeded in making his escape into the brush, where he spent the night, and came into camp the next day with six bullet wounds on his person.

The rest of the party fortunately got off unharmed, having to abandon the train in charge, which the *banditti* disposed off by shooting the six mules and burning the wagon, after taking therefrom such things as they could appropriate; an opportunity which they never overlooked, as they invariably stripped whenever they could get a chance.

Meanwhile, in and around Independence, they continued their fiendish work, killing all men (who would not join in their barbarity) without discrimination. On the twenty-ninth of April, a detachment of our troops under command of Lieutenant Spencer, pursued on the trail of a party of bushwhackers between Lone Jack and the Sni Hills. Coming up with them they charged them, but the bandits were well mounted, as they took care no one should have a good horse if it suited them. The horses of two of the boys had borne them far in advance of the others, which proved fatal to them, killing one and wounding the other.

The one who fell dead at the first fire was George Wells, private of Company K; the other was John Freestone, of Company G, who was severely wounded. On the thirteenth of June, Sergeant-Major Hennion with an escort of eight men and a six-mule team in charge, was attacked about five o'clock in the afternoon about four miles south west of Westport, on the Hickman's Mill road, by a band of twenty-five or thirty bushwhackers under the infamous *desperado*, Dick Yager. The first volley fired, although not over twenty feet distant, had no other effect than the wounding of Hennion slightly in the ankle and the complete surprise of our little party, who fired several hurried shots and took to the brush, closely pursued.

At the second discharge from the enemy Hennion's horse was killed and the cylinder blown from his revolver at the same time; but he succeeded in making his escape into the brush, where he lay until ten o'clock that night and reached Kansas City the next morning at six o'clock with three bullet holes in his jacket and one through his pants. The rest of the party succeeded in getting away unharmed. Two of them who were in advance hastened forward to Hickman's Mill for reinforcements, and one of the party set out during the night and reached Hickman's Mill next day. The *banditti* captured the team, unloaded some goods belonging to Mrs. Johnson, of Company L, and directed her to a house nearby where she could stay until relief would come. They then set fire to the wagon, killed two of the mules and wounded a third, which they left; the other three they appropriated to their own use. Some days afterward a fresh grave was found near the spot, supposed to be that of a bushwhacker killed in the encounter.

The frequency of these attacks and the increasing temerity of the assassins required energetic action on the part of our troops, consequently Colonel Ford ordered the regiment into the field and established its headquarters near a deserted village called Kaytown, situated on the Independence and Hickman's Mill road, and sixteen miles distant from Kansas City. From this point the troops, under Majors Smith and Pritchard and other officers of the regiment; scoured the country in every direction, sometimes mounted and at other times dismounted, which had the desired effect of driving the marauders from that portion of the country to seek a safer and more congenial latitude. During one of these scouts, Corporal Martin, of Company H, with ten men, some two miles east of camp, were quietly passing along, when hearing a noise as if some persons were talking in the distance, quickly concealed themselves in the brush.

Our party awaited the approach of the other party, who coming within fifty yards were discovered to be bushwhackers, five in number, and were immediately fired upon by the scout. A ball from the gun of Private Jones, of Company H, passed through the hip of one of the enemy named Young, wounding him severely, but his horse carried him off. Pursuing the course taken by them and coming up to a house, the alarm was given by someone who acted as sentinel, and out rushed the same party and after a hurried exchange of shots disappeared in the brush. Young, the wounded man, was killed a short time afterward. Headquarters of the regiment remained at Raytown about one month, during which time the troops were kept constantly on the move.

Various expedients were resorted to to entrap the enemy, but they had become aware of the dangerous locality and quietly decamped until a more favourable opportunity presented itself. As they were always on the alert such opportunity was not long wanting. They were always ready to jump out from behind a fence corner or an old cabin and shoot down in cold blood the unwary, in evidence of which on the twenty-sixth day of May, Thomas Herrington and William Ford, the latter known as Pat Ford (in the regiment), both privates of Company A, were detailed to carry express from Hickman's Mill to Pleasant Hill and back. On their return trip when a few miles from Pleasant Hill, a messenger dressed in Federal uniform halted them just as they turned to pass a heavy thicket of brush. Laying his hand on the bridle of one of the horses, he said he had orders for them to return to Pleasant Hill for some dispatches that had been omitted. Not thinking it was a ruse to take them at a disadvantage they listened unguardedly, when, in an instant, several more made their appearance.

They found out when too late they were in the hands of the most villainous cut-throats. On seeing how they were entrapped they raised their guns to fire, but were immediately covered with six or eight revolvers in the hands of the enemy, who assured them if they would surrender they should not be harmed. They then took their horses, arms and dispatches, and after holding them prisoners for a few hours they shot them down in cold blood. Thomas Herrington seemed to have been shot without warning; the ball passed through the head and he apparently died without a struggle. William Ford had evidently fought hard for his life, for he had many wounds in his head and shoulders. Poor boys! theirs was a sad fate. They were beloved and regretted by all their comrades. Their bodies were taken to Pleasant Hill, and the ladies of that town kindly performed the last sad duties for them and decorated their graves with flowers.

> *They brought the fairest flowerets, the brightest flowers that bloom,*
> *To deck our comrade's clay-cold brows, to deck our comrade's tomb;*
> *We never shall forget the hands, the kindly ones which gave*
> *That last kind tribute to the dead, to deck with flowers their grave.*
> *We loved them, we've stood side by side 'mid cannon's deafening rattle,*
> *And bore our stars and banner on through many a hard fought battle;*
> *We loved them, they were dear to us as brother is to brother,*
> *For soldiers in this war and strife grow dear to one another.*
> *Two fathers long, aye, long ago in earthly beds were sleeping;*
> *Two mothers dear are left alone and for their loved ones weeping;*

What calm each mother's heart to know that woman's gentle care
Hath gazed upon their forms and placed the beauteous blossoms there.

The soldier's heart is gushing full of gratitude and love,
They only hope to meet with such angelic forms above;
Their blessings rest upon the brows of those, the good and fair, Who placed the early flowers of spring upon their comrade's bier.

C. Williams, Co. A.

Chapter 5

Bushwacked

A few days previous to this sad occurrence, on the tenth day of May, Lieutenant Gooding with twenty men of Companies H and G started from Pleasant Hill after night had set in on a scout of three days' duration; on the night of the second day out, while scouting twenty miles north-east of Pleasant Hill, they drew up to a house owned by one named Webb. Upon entering, although past eleven o'clock, the table was found ready "set" and every necessary preparation made for a meal; upon inquiry, our party was informed that there was no bushwhackers in the country, but not being inclined to give credence to the smooth tongues and unqualified assertions of the "war-widows," who were so numerous in that portion of the country and who could live there unmolested while depredations were being committed all around them our boys kept a sharp lookout, and after leaving the house and proceeding cautiously along the road some three miles, they were met by a party of four men, who were just emerging from the brush and could barely be discerned in the darkness of the night. "Who are you?" challenged their leader.

"Who are you?" demanded Gooding, while every man grasped his revolver with a firmer grip. Without deigning to give answer the four men wheeled about, put spurs to their horses and fled through the thick under-brush, amid a shower of bullets from the well directed fire of the advance. The next day the dead bodies of two of the bandits were found near the scene of the encounter.

During the campaign a portion of the troops had been stationed at Camp Smith, some three miles south-west of Independence, and, on the sixth of July, Captain S. Wagoner, of Company C, and twenty-five of his men left camp and proceeded in a north-easterly direction until reaching the Pleasant Hill and Independence road, about eight miles distant from the latter mentioned place; here they saw four men who immediately took to flight, and while pursuing them our party was charged upon by nearly one hundred bushwhackers, who were lying in ambush awaiting their approach.

Unconscious of the presence of so large a body of the foe until they rushed forth from the dense thicket, with savage yells that would have done credit to a parcel of redskins, and poured a deadly volley into the midst of the scouts, who, nothing daunted, firmly stood their ground, and, with their brave captain leading them on, returned the fire, although outnumbered four to one by the foe, who came rushing on until the combatants were mingled together, fighting a hand-to-hand encounter midst the fallen dead and dying. The gallant Wagoner fell, mortally wounded, and dragging himself a few feet to one side he gave a farewell shot, that sent an enemy reeling to the ground with his life blood spurting from the wound, and shouted, "Give them death, boys," and breathed his last. Completely overpowered by numbers our troops were forced to fall back and surrender the field to the enemy, with the loss of their valiant captain and seven brave men killed and one wounded. The loss of the enemy was nine killed and fifteen wounded.

They took the arms and what money was on the persons of our boys and left their bodies lying as they fell, where a strong force of our troops who were sent out found them, and brought them to Independence the next morning and buried them in a body in the cemetery with a brick wall surrounding the entire number; and the company, assisted by the officers of the regiment, erected a fine marble monument to mark their resting-place. I was requested to write an inscription and in answer I wrote the following which was inscribed on the monument erected in the cemetery at Independence, in Missouri:

> *Brave heroes rest beneath this sculptured stone;*
> *In unfair contest slain by murderous hands.*
> *They knew no yielding to a cruel foe*
> *And thus, this tribute to their memory stands*
> *Our country's honour, and a nation's pride*
> *'Twas thus they nobly lived and bravely died.*

Captain Wagoner was a brave man, of which his surviving comrades were ready to testify. His loss and that of the brave men who fell with him cast a gloom over the entire regiment.

Notwithstanding the increased vigilance of our troops in scouring the country in search of these brigands, it was seldom they caught them "napping," for they were cognizant of the danger they were incurring by remaining in the country and committing their depredations, and were cautious of their movements; only making a demonstration when assured of success on their part. Being intimately acquainted with the entire country (having resided there for years) and having the advantage of acting on the defensive, when our troops were sent in pursuit of them, they for a long time succeeded in evading an open collision with them, feeling uninclined to extend their acquaintance with men who gave them such a rough introduction.

About this time a *desperado* by the name of Thornton came into the counties on the north side of the river, and was collecting together all the bushwhackers and other vagabonds that would flock to his standard, in order to go into offensive operations against the Union people on a large scale and finally escape to the Southern army, as it was getting rather warm for their comfort and safety.

Through the spies he had employed to watch the movements of the enemy, Colonel Ford learned of their place of rendezvous, and about two o'clock in the morning of the thirteenth of July, he quietly embarked on board the *Fanny Ogden*, and the *Emilie*, with about three hundred men, in the midst of a heavy rainstorm, and proceeded as far as Weston, a town on the north bank of the Missouri River, about seven miles above Leavenworth City, landing at this point the troops bivouacked, until twelve o'clock in the morning, and being reinforced by a portion of the Sixteenth Kansas Cavalry, under Colonel Jennison, the column moved toward Camden Point, a town of one hundred and fifty inhabitants, arriving within four miles of the town our advance encountered the rebel pickets, who hastily fired a volley and retreated, pursued by the advance who succeeded in killing two of their number; the others made their escape into the thick brush on the roadside: the brigade was formed in fours, and the order "gallop" was given and the column moved forward at a rapid rate, over the road, Company F (Captain West) leading the advance; on arriving at the town, the rebels were found drawn up in line about three hundred and fifty strong, ready for battle; Captain West also formed his men in line at hailing distance and demanded, "Who are you?"

The question was reiterated by the rebel leader. West replied, "Captain West, of the Second Colorado."

The reply came back, proud and defiant, "We do not recognize Captain West and his party," and the rebel colours were immediately displayed. Captain West instantly ordered a charge, and the rebel ranks were broken and scattered by the fierce onset of our troops; who bore down on the foe like an avalanche, sweeping all before them, amid the smoke and din of battle, and the wild, deafening cheers of our men, that rang out loud and clear upon the air, and was echoed and re-echoed through the surrounding forest, the rebel forces, after exchanging a few volleys, fled in every direction in the wildest confusion, in many instances leaving their horses and equipments, and quite a number throwing down their arms, taking to the brush pursued closely by our troops, who having become exasperated by their former fiendishness, shot them down like so many dogs without mercy.

The main portion fled on the road leading east of the town, and were hotly pursued for nearly five miles, but being mounted on fresh horses they finally escaped and our troops returned and camped on the same ground occupied previously by their forces. Our loss was one man killed (Private Flannegan) and one wounded (Sergeant Crane), both of Company F; that of the rebels was twenty-one killed, if any were wounded they made their escape.

In this action the rebel colours, which was presented to them by the ladies of Platte City and bore the motto "*Protect Missouri,*" was captured by Company F. The next day Colonel Ford's command pushed forward in the direction of Platte City, a small town about eight miles south-east of Camden Point, containing some three or four hundred inhabitants, and noted for being a place of rendezvous for bushwhackers and rebels. A small rebel sheet had been published here, supported by the citizens of the town and the surrounding country, flourishing under the title of The Platte City Register. The command arrived here about ten o'clock in the morning, camped and remained until next day, with the exception of Company K, under Lieutenant Parsons, which continued on the trail of the remnant of the party of bushwhackers who were defeated at Camden Point.

On the morning of the fifteenth, Colonel Ford and his command moved toward Liberty, the county seat of Clay County, where they arrived at two o'clock in the afternoon and went into camp. Headquarters remaining at this place for several days, detachments in the meantime were sent out to various portions of the surrounding country, at different times, in order to intercept any small parties of bushwhackers that might be prowling about, and also to get any information of the whereabouts of Thornton's gang, who were supposed to be collecting again for the purpose of making their escape out of the country. On the twenty-first of the month, about forty men belonging to the Second Colorado, in charge of Lieutenant Hammond, of the Seventh Missouri, proceeded from Kansas City according to instructions from Colonel Ford, to join his command at Liberty. Upon arriving at this place the command had already gone, proceeding north on the Plattsburg road, instructions having been left for the reinforcements under Lieutenant Hammond to follow the command.

Hastily feeding the horses, allowing them but a few minutes to rest, at four o'clock in the afternoon we were in the saddle again on the road to Plattsburg, moving at a lively walk and frequently breaking into a long, steady gallop, while the dust arose in clouds, covering the horses already wet with perspiration, and clothing the riders with so dense a coating that their countenances were barely distinguish able.

About eleven o'clock at night we reached a house on the roadside, within six miles of Plattsburg, where the detachment halted for water and to make inquiries concerning Colonel Ford's command. Upon hailing the inmates of the house, who had retired, a female voice replied by asking who we were. Lieutenant Hammond replied, "We are soldiers and want to speak to you, if you will come to the door," to which no reply was given. Awaiting a sufficient length of time and no one appearing the lieutenant called the second time, assuring them no harm should befall them, but that he only wanted to make some inquiries; but no response being given he ordered them to open the door or he would break it down.

Upon this being threatened a stir was heard inside and a window was suddenly thrown open on the rear of the house, and a man in his night-dress sprang to the ground and bounded into a dense grove of locust bushes nearby, closely grazed by a ball from the carbine of one of the party. His exit was unexpected, and, consequently, unprepared for. The moment the shrill report of the gun rang upon the still night air a series of piercing screams issued from within the building, the females supposing the rifle had done its work. The soldiers sprang from their saddles and clearing the fence pursued the direction taken by the fugitive, but under cover of the darkness of the night he succeeded in escaping in an adjacent cornfield.

Disappointed in not securing the man and exasperated at their refusal to come forth, the lieutenant returned to the house, which by this time had been broken open, and in no very mild terms assured the inmates consisting of three women that for their obstinate conduct in refusing to open the door, and also secreting a bushwhacker, they richly merited the burning of the house to the ground, whereas, had they complied with his request, they would have been unmolested.

The house was searched, but no arms were found and the party mounted their horses and passed on. Marching on some three miles further the command drew up to a house by the roadside, and upon inquiry, learned that Colonel Ford's command had left the road and marched across the country toward Gosnerville, a small place some sixteen miles distant and in a westerly direction; the horses being very much fatigued and the men wearied with the long ride and the want of sleep, and it being almost impossible to follow the trail by starlight, Lieutenant Hammond thought it best to halt and rest till daylight; securing the horses and scaling the fence, the boys soon plucked oats enough to feed the somewhat jaded animals, and throwing out a picket guard they threw themselves upon the ground with their saddles for pillows and were soon fast asleep, from which they were awakened by the shrill notes of the bugle at early dawn.

Feeling considerably refreshed by the two hours rest and sleep, they hastily saddled their horses, mounted and were soon on the trail that led through a wild untenanted part of the country. About ten o'clock the party reached Gosnerville, where they learned that the command had proceeded in the direction of Platte City, leaving orders for Lieutenant Hammond to return with his force to Liberty, which they did, arriving at that point about three o'clock the same evening; having travelled over one hundred miles in a few hours. Upon leaving Liberty, Colonel Ford proceeded north on the Plattsburg road about twenty-five miles, where a trail was discovered leading in the direction of Gosnerville, which he immediately followed, and arrived at the latter mentioned place about four o'clock in the afternoon; here the trail was lost, and getting no information as to the direction taken he pushed forward in a westerly direction some three miles where the command was halted.

The horses fed and rested until darkness approached, when

the bugle sounded boots and saddles, and in a few minutes the battalion was moving.

Marching some four miles a halt was ordered, and the men lay down and slept soundly in the open air until three o'clock in the morning, when they were again on the move, and by one o'clock in the afternoon reached Camden Point without meeting the foe; here they changed direction to the south and marching some eight miles then camped.

The next morning the colonel was up long before day, and the battalion was soon mounted and moving on toward the south-west. After passing over some ten miles of ground without any road, they suddenly came upon a fresh trail of a party of twenty-five or thirty bushwhackers, and immediately joined in the pursuit, which was kept up until three o'clock that afternoon, when arriving at a house owned by a rebel by the name of Woods they halted to feed and make inquiries; but, although the trail had been followed to the door-yard, the inmates could tell nothing in regard to them; but a few minutes had elapsed, when a man came out of the brush and entered our lines, evidently under the impression that our forces be longed to rebel Stone's party; discovering his mistake he put spurs to his horse and dashed past at a gallop under a shower of balls, but finally fell from his horse pierced by a dozen bullets.

Mounting their horses our troops scoured the woods, and discovered a camp within half a mile that had just been deserted, having been alarmed by the firing; our troops immediately started in pursuit and on emerging from the timber discovered a party of mounted men numbering twenty about one mile in advance and flying at the top of their speed; raising a shout our boys dashed after them over the open prairie and were fast gaining ground when the bushwhackers again entered the timber and scattering were again lest to view in the dense underbrush that covered the ground; the trail was followed for eight miles through the timber and ravines, when the pickets of the bushwhackers' camp were again discovered.

Upon hailing them they replied that they belonged to Stone's command, they were fired upon by our boys, who succeeded in killing one man and wounding another, the rest of the bandits made their escape.

CHAPTER 6

Operations Against Prices Invasion

About the nineteenth of July, Major Smith, in command of about one hundred and forty men, left Liberty and proceeded to Richfield, a small town south of Liberty and fourteen miles distant, situated on the Missouri River; on going into town the advance guard discovered and fired upon a party of bushwhackers, some thirty strong, who beat a hasty retreat; taking their trail the command pursued them for eight miles down the river; here Major Smith divided his forces; about fifty men under Captain Green, taking the road back towards Richfield for the purpose of intercepting any of the enemy who might have taken the back track; another party of about forty under his own command pursued a north-east direction, while Captain Moses, with forty-seven men belonging to Companies M and C, pursued an easterly direction seven or eight miles and camped.

The next morning his party were mounted and pushing forward, about one o'clock in the afternoon, they arrived at a little town by the name of Fredericksburg, situated in Bay County and some twenty miles distant from Liberty; upon nearing the town a body of troops were discovered to be approaching from an opposite direction, at first they were supposed to be a portion of our own forces, under Major Smith; but that illusion was quickly dispelled by a volley of shots coming from their advance; not in the least disconcerted, Captain Moses instantly dismounted the first platoon and formed them in line across the road in front and returned a deadly fire on the foe, which had the effect to check their advancing columns, although their vastly out numbering rifles rained a perfect shower of leaden messengers of death in the midst of our little band, who firmly, heroically, stood their ground, and returned shot for shot and volley for volley, telling fearfully on the ranks of the enemy and holding them at bay, although more than five times their number, until the horses that had been pressed by our party—and of which they had a large number—became frightened and, consequently, unmanageable, rearing and plunging until they threw our little band into confusion, which was taken advantage of by Thrailkill, leader of the enemy; and throwing out his flankers on both sides of the road, he with the main body charged down the lane upon our confused but dauntless heroes, who met the foe in deadly combat, hand-to-hand, sternly contesting the field, some of them mounted and some on foot; the terrific plunging of the horses, unused to the field and consequent confusion, not allowing them an opportunity to mount before the enemy were upon them.

For the space of twenty minutes—which seemed as so many hours—the fight raged in all its fury, and the ground was strewn with the wounded, dying and dead; some of our men, who had fallen mortally wounded, fighting while the life-blood was spurting from their wounds even to the death; but on they came, yelling like so many demons, swarming from the woods. Captain Moses who was in the thickest of the fight, seeing the utter hopelessness of con tending with such great odds, directed his men to save themselves and they reluctantly dispersed and taking to the woods escaped—after being hotly pursued for over a mile—leaving six of their number dead on the field.

Both the captain and his men behaved with the greatest coolness and bravery; the former came off the field with three bullet marks on his clothes and person, one ball grazing his forehead cutting the skin slightly, another severed his sabre-belt and a third cutting his coat; his horse, a noble animal, was pierced by three balls, but carried him out of all danger. Nearly every one of the party who escaped with their lives bore some evidence of the desperate contest, either upon his clothes or his person; several of the horses were killed and several were wounded; all the led horses were lost, escaping in their mad fright in every direction, fleeing for their lives in wild consternation.

After the fight was over our men, who had considerable experience in hunting bushwhackers, immediately scattered through the woods each one taking his own course, thereby eluding the pursuit of the exasperated and blood-thirsty enemy, and each making his way into camp as soon as time and circumstance would permit; in so doing many dangers were to be avoided and many narrow escapes had to be run. The first messengers from the scene of action arrived at Liberty at about half-past four o'clock in the afternoon, and about one hundred men, under command of Lieutenant Gooding, were ordered to the rescue.

Having saddled and mounted, the command "forward" was given, and letting their horses out into a long gallop they moved forward at a rapid gait toward the scene of the contest, each man eager to meet and chastise severely the cowardly fiends who would risk a fight only when conscious of an advantage in their favour; just as night was setting in, and when within about six miles of the battle-ground, they were met by two more of our men, who had been in the brush during the latter part of the day and only ventured forth when it became dark enough to cover their movement from any of the enemy who might be watching for their appearance; the men gave a detailed account of the fight and stated, what proved afterward to be a fact, that the enemy were near three hundred strong, and were doubt less on the alert for reinforcements that would in all probability be sent by our commander.

Taking into consideration the darkness of the night, the dense forest and broken country through which they would be obliged to pass, and the advantage the enemy would possess in numbers and position, the commanding officer decided to halt the command and send a messenger back for additional reinforcements. The dispatch bearer arrived safe at Liberty, and Major Pritchard with one hundred and fifty mounted men joined the command at about half-past one o'clock in the morning, when the entire body, near two hundred and fifty strong, under command of the major, moved forward to the scene of the previous day's fight, having taken the precaution to throw out flankers, for a considerable distance on each side of the road.

At about four o'clock the battle ground was reached, and from citizens who lived near it was ascertained that the enemy had moved forward after stripping the dead of their arms, money and clothing—whom the citizens had collected and deposited in a church nearby, preparatory to interment—they also stated the number of the enemy killed in the engagement to be sixteen, having helped to bury them; the number of wounded was not ascertained. The command moved forward on the road until daylight when a halt was ordered and the somewhat jaded horses were fed from an adjacent cornfield, the saddles remaining upon them and the bits in their mouths.

Having rested a short time, the command was mounted and moving forward over the road for some three miles; the trail of the enemy was discovered to diverge to the right and, pursuing the direction taken, their camp-ground was found on a river bottom, but had been deserted by them about an hour previous. Again taking up the trail our troops wound their way through the forest and thick underbrush and emerged into the road, having lost considerable ground in following the trail; moving on to within three miles of Richmond, the country seat of Ray County, the trail again diverged to the left, but not wishing to lose any more time, the major and command dashed straight forward into the place and waited the coming up of the enemy, who was supposed to have taken a circuitous route for the purpose of throwing their pursuers off the scent; in the meantime, a scout having been sent out to reconnoitre, returned and reported the enemy having pushed on in an easterly direction. Taking up a line of march our troops once more struck their trail about four miles distant, about an hour and a half after they had passed.

In pursuing the course taken by the enemy, it was necessary

to exercise caution in order to avoid being ambushed by the foe, which might prove fatal to our party; and in order to guard against this, Major Pritchard threw out flanks for a considerable distance on each side of the road, who were compelled to pick their way through the dense underbrush, through fences and over logs, ravines and hillocks, necessarily causing tardy movements on the part of our forces.

Pursuing the trail for about five miles farther they came to the ground where the enemy had camped and fed their horses; but had moved on sometime before our troops came up, according to information obtained from citizens on the road, who seemed anxious to impart anything they knew that would be of service to our troops in their endeavours to over haul the enemy. When within three miles of the town of Knoxville, the dead body of a citizen was found lying by the roadside—killed by the *banditti*—and on pushing on two miles farther a large amount of destroyed mail matter was found on the road, where the coach had been plundered and the mail bags rifled and their contents strewn over the ground; being within one mile of the town the major ordered a charge and the battalion moved forward at a gallop, with drawn revolvers.

Upon reaching Knoxville the birds had flown, much to the chagrin and disappointment of our troops, who were anxious to give them a severe chastisement for their many evil deeds committed through that country. Moving in advance of our column the enemy had the advantage of securing all the best horses in the country, such an opportunity they never failed to improve, and by so doing could bid defiance to the pursuers, whose horses had well nigh given out—having travelled over one hundred miles with very little rest. Taking into consideration the wearied men and the jaded condition of the horses, the major deemed it advisable to give over the pursuit and return to camp, which after a brief halt was carried into effect—the command reaching Liberty that night. In service of this nature, it was impossible to have wagons at all times for the transportation of subsistence and the troops were obliged—along with what provisions they carried in their haversacks—to subsist upon the farmers throughout the country, who had abundance of everything required; nor were our men slow to help themselves to what they needed to satisfy their appetites while passing through a country whose inhabitants were so notoriously rebel in their sentiments and actions.

Up to the time of the invasion by our troops, they had never experienced the evil effects of war brought to their own doors, and while the counties of Jackson, Cass, Bates and others across the river, suffered all the terrible consequences of being overrun and devastated by the contending forces, they had reaped all the benefits of the scarcity of provisions in the market and consequent rise in prices; at the same time allowed the secession element to flourish unmolested in their midst, until it manifested itself in such gigantic magnitude that it became intolerable and had to be crushed. And now, having the war brought to their own doors and realizing some of its blighting effects, they were obliged to take measures for their own peace and safety. Meetings were held and resolutions passed, and bodies of men were organized to keep down bushwhacking and preserve order throughout the country, preferring to take the matter into their own hands rather than have their country laid waste by the soldiers, who had but little reason to show leniency to the rebels against the United States Government and still less for the bushwhackers.

Matters having become quiet and somewhat settled in that part of the country, Colonel Ford and command returned to Kansas City, after assuring the people of Clay County that very severe measures might be expected should he be obliged to pay them another visit.

About the twentieth of September, General Sterling Price, with a cavalry force some twenty thousand strong, invaded Missouri from the south, meeting with but little opposition until reaching Pilot Knob—a small town of about four hundred inhabitants, situated in Iron county at the terminus of the Iron Mountain Railroad and eighty-six miles south from St. Louis—

where he arrived on the twenty-seventh day of September, and immediately commenced an attack on the Fort at that place, garrisoned by about eight hundred men under command of General Ewing.

The attack began at six o'clock in the morning and lasted until dark, our gallant little band foiling the repeated attempts of the enemy to take the place, repulsing their vastly outnumbering forces with tremendous slaughter. The fort was *septangular* in form, with earthworks thrown up to the height of nine feet, and ten feet in thickness, and surrounded by a deep ditch with almost perpendicular sides, from which the earth was taken to raise the embankments. It was compactly built and mounted seven guns in all, four thirty two pound siege-guns and three twenty-four pound field-pieces, also, two mortars of six-inch calibre for throwing bombs. The magazine was located underground in the centre of the fort, and one twenty-four pound gun mounted upon its roof, which was of solid earth four feet in depth, to protect the ammunition from the effect of the enemy's fire.

On the south-west side of the fort was the passage-way leading outside into the rifle-pits, that were dug for the protection of our marksmen while disputing the passage of the enemy to the right and rear of the defences. The enemy made several successive charges, but were repulsed each time leaving many of their number dead on the field.

Our loss during the day was ten killed and twenty-one wounded. The entire loss of the rebels reached near fifteen hundred! Nearly twice the number of the garrison! This terrible slaughter was accounted for by the fact that the guns were so arranged that their fire could be concentrated on any given point, and as the columns advanced they were greeted with a most deadly reception, in the shape of shot, shell, grape and canister, that utterly mowed the enemy down and caused utter confusion in their broken ranks.

At dark Price drew off his forces to Arcadia, a small town two miles and a half below, intending to make a combined effort to take the fort by assault the next day. General Ewing not having received any reinforce ments, and knowing it would be impossible to hold out for a much longer period against such fearful odds, wisely removed our dead and wounded and such property as could not be abandoned, and evacuating at half-past two o'clock in the night, blew up the fortifications and retired, and the place was occupied by the rebel forces next day.

Exasperated at our stubborn and successful resistance and their severe loss in the action, the rebels wreaked their vengeance upon the Union citizens living in the vicinity, by entering their houses and appropriating such of the articles contained in them, that they coveted, to their own use and destroying the remainder, and in some instances burning the houses to the ground.

In the meantime General Ewing retreated in good order in a north-westerly direction, leaving the enemy in possession of the Iron Mountain Railroad running to St. Louis, care having been taken to remove the rolling stock, thus rendering it useless to the enemy as a means of conveyance to the city or intermediate points. The object of the invasion of the rebel army was to ascertain the number and to collect together all who were willing to fight under the rebel colours, and if possible hold the State as belonging to the rebel Confederacy. From numerous letters written in different parts of the State, the commander of the rebel force had assurances that a large number of rebel residents were only awaiting an opportunity to fall into line and march to the music of secession.

These representations, together with a strong desire to regain the foothold he once had in the State, and the faint hope of bring Missouri again under the rule of the so-called "Southern Confederacy," also for the purpose of dividing the attention of our Government, thereby weakening its attempts to put down the rebellion, were the inducements that offered themselves to the consideration of General Price; and finally resulted in the "great raid" during the months of October and November. The results of which proved such a failure to the designs of the rebel leader.

While Price with his augmenting force, was pushing his way through the State, in a north west direction, all sorts of vague rumours in regard to the rebel general, his designs and the numerical strength of his forces, were flying over the country, creating considerable excitement and consternation among the Union citizens residing on the line of his march; and rejoicing among the rebel portion of residents throughout the State.

Upon receipt of intelligence of the approach of the rebel army, General Curtis, then commanding the department of Kansas, immediately forwarded dispatches to the department at Washington, stating the necessity of concentrating a strong force on the border, urging immediate action in regard to the matter, and asking to be supplied with a sufficient body of troops to repel the invading force and capture or drive the enemy from the country, and avert the impending danger of its being overrun and devastated by a relentless foe, who would have gloried in the act of carrying fire and sword into the heart of loyal Kansas, and desecrating the homes and firesides of the freemen who had battled so long and successfully against the foes of liberty and human freedom.

The Second Colorado had just been ordered to report to the Kansas Department for active service against the Indians, who had assumed a hostile attitude toward the whites, capturing trains, running stock and killing any small parties of travellers that were so unfortunate as to fall into their merciless clutches. A portion of the regiment was at Leavenworth when, on the eighteenth of October, the proclamation of martial law was prepared. The Second immediately took the field and for several days before General Blunt moved toward Lexington, Colonel Ford, from Independence, was scouring the country thoroughly. The much lamented Major Smith entered and left Lexington the day before General Blunt's reconnoitring column.

On the twelfth of October, while headquarters of the regiment was at Kansas City, the excitement of that place had become so great in regard to the coming of the rebel Price and the prospect of his paying the city a visit, that Major Pritchard, who was at that time in command of the post, ordered all business houses to be closed that afternoon at four o'clock, and the citizens to turn out to drill and prepare to meet the enemy. A survey was made and rifle-pits dug, extending from the bank of the river on the east of the city to the south west portion, protecting the approaches from Independence on the east and Westport on the south. To accomplish this, every man who was able to wield a pick or shovel and who was not already on duty drilling was ordered to the entrenchments.

Determined to enforce the order without fear or favour, Major Pritchard placed the entire company of Squadron H on provost duty, with instructions to find and convey to the trenches all idlers and shirkers from duty. As a matter of course the loyal portion of the citizens needed no urging, the necessity of the occasion being sufficient incentive for them; but it was gratifying to the soldiers to get after the "sympathizers" and stay-at-home rebs of whom the city and vicinity possessed a large number, who were too cowardly to openly espouse the cause of the rebels, but chose rather to remain at home out of the way of bullets and gunpowder and discourage Union sentiments and feelings by their contaminating influence and intolerable hypocrisy; of which some of their leading characters possessed this contemptible quality to a most astonishing and alarming extent.

Some characters in particular, who wore very meek countenances and had tongues that for oily smoothness, when in company with Union men, might be likened unto never-failing fountains of kerosene, and yet were known to be deep-dyed rebels at heart, made themselves particularly obnoxious. These characters were well known to the soldiery and received their particular attention. As the rebel army continued its march through the State rumours of every description were circulated, causing great excitement and an almost total suspension of business.

Chapter 7
Death of Major Smith

The Union citizens of Independence, a town of about one thousand five hundred inhabitants, situated nine miles east of Kansas City, deeming it unsafe to remain longer at that place, evacuated it on the evening of the twelfth of October, and reached Kansas City that night.

On the morning of the thirteenth, the railroad bridge across the Big Blue, between Independence and the latter mentioned place, was burned by a band of bushwhackers, and Captain Moses of the Second Colorado, in command of companies M and C, anticipating a design on the part of the enemy to cut off his retreat, abandoned Independence where he had been stationed and fell back to Kansas City. The afternoon of the same day, information reached us that Independence had been taken possession of by the bushwhackers and was being pillaged by the relentless vagabonds.

Hastily collecting together about one hundred and twenty-five men, Captain Moses proceeded to that place by the river-road; when within about three miles of the place, the command was met by a man who informed Captain Moses that the town was full of rebels—the advance of Price's army. Drawing his men up in line and giving them instructions in case of an engagement with the enemy, the captain ordered the column for ward, keeping clear of the road to avoid being ambushed. Upon arriving within one mile a party was sent out to reconnoitre while the command quietly dismounted to rest a few moments; failing to get satisfactory information the command was mounted and moved silently forward until within a quarter of a mile, when a charge was ordered and the column went sweeping for ward like the resistless hurricane, each one firmly impressed with the conviction that the enemy were posted in strong force in the town.

Charging down the hard, stony street at the top of their speed, the clatter of the horses hoofs rang loud and clear, and as the column drew up on the public square, alarmed citizens might be seen rushing into their houses terrified at the sudden appearance of our troops; but, they arrived too late; some twenty-five bushwhackers had visited the town and appropriating what articles they wanted immediately decamped with their booty, having been gone about one hour previous to the arrival of our troops. Remaining in town until night set in, Captain Moses and command started for Hickman's Mills; when within about five miles of that place, they were met by Major Smith, with two hundred men; after a few minutes consultation the entire force under command of the major returned to Independence.

On arriving within one mile of the town, the rear of the command, consisting of about two hundred men, took the road to the right to come in on another street, in order to intercept the flight of any bushwhackers who might have entered the town and would endeavour to make their escape, of which movement the advance being some distance ahead were entirely ignorant, and which might have proved disastrous in its consequences had less discretion been used afterwards. Our advance had just entered the street running north and on the west side of the public square when by the dim starlight two mounted men were seen standing in the street near the square, apparently watching our movements.

Upon our approach to within three hundred yards they suddenly disappeared down the street running west, as if conscious of the near advance of a superior force. This suspicious movement and the threat that the bushwhackers gave utterance to that day—that they would return to town that night, strongly reinforced, for the purpose of burning and sacking the place—had the effect to assure them that they had at last "treed" their game, and the exultant ejaculation, "Boys, we've got them now," quickly passed from front to rear as the command "Forward" was given and the battalion went thundering over the stone-paved street, while a squad dashed off to the right to come in on the street running parallel on the east side of the square, for the purpose of intercepting the enemy in their flight should they conclude that discretion were the better part of valour and try to make their escape.

Coming up at a lively gallop a large number of men with horses were seen gathered around the square, as though they felt themselves masters of the town and dreaded not the approach of the troops. Dashing up to within twenty-five yards, the darkness of the night rendering it impossible to distinguish anything more than the outlines of the figures moving about, the command was halted, and half a dozen excited voices from the ranks of the Colorados simultaneously rang out with, "Who are you?"

"Who are you?" came back the reply, proud and defiant. "Come out and make yourselves known," was the answer, as the click of a hundred revolvers was heard on the still night air. Each one was almost fully assured the enemy was there in strong force and momentarily expected to receive a deadly volley from their ranks. At this juncture, while the excitement was at its height, one of their party advanced and was met by one of the other, when after a brief consultation it was ascertained that they were a portion of their own troops, who had taken the road to the right and had arrived in advance of the battalion under Captain Moses, So fully were the troops impressed with the belief that they were in the presence of an enemy that some seconds passed before they could realize the true state of the case; and when fully satisfied in regard to the matter, a thrill of horror chilled the blood of the entire command to think how nearly fatal had been their mistake.

Accustomed to guerrilla warfare, and realizing by experience the fact that they often opened fire upon our own forces without extended explanations, and also aware of the ruse frequently practiced by them, that of claiming to be Colorado troops, it was a matter of astonishment to the entire command that they did not open fire upon hearing the sullen and unsatisfactory reply of the other party.

It really seemed that nothing short of the hand of Providence intervened to prevent the flow of blood! The cold-blooded and inhuman murder of some of our men by the bushwhackers, and the consequent rule of no "quarter," adopted by our troops when contending with them, had begotten a feeling of animosity between the two forces that speedily ripened into a deadly feud; and when a struggle between the two belligerent parties did ensue it was for life or death!

In the present instance, had one shot been fired a scene, with its terrible results, would have ensued that would beggar all attempts at description. Amid the clash and clanging of sabres and the incessant roar of firearms, mingled with the shouts of the combatants, each fully assured that they were fully engaged with their mortal enemy, it would have been utterly impossible, in the darkness of the night to have discovered the terrible error, until too late to save the lives of a large number of our brave boys, whose mettle had been tried and whose courage was unquestioned.

But fortunately for the command the threatened danger was averted, and, it being after midnight, they turned into quarters, after having a strong picket guard placed upon all the roads leading to the town, with strict orders to keep a vigilant watch for the enemy, whose appearance was hourly expected. The next morning at an early hour the assembly was blown, and in a few minutes the command was mounted and moved forward on the road leading to Lexington for the purpose of reconnoitring. Passing over some twenty miles of the road and discovering no evidence of the proximity of the foe, Major Smith left the road, and after proceeding in a northerly direction four or five miles the command was halted, and the horses were fed from an adjacent cornfield.

After resting a few minutes the troops moved on in the direction of the Sni Hills; a rough, rocky, broken part of the country, densely covered with brush and noted for being a rendezvous for the bushwhackers, who, when they had once succeeded in escaping into this region, it was a dangerous and generally unwarrantable experiment for our troops to endeavour to ferret them out of their stronghold.

Bearing to the right and striking the Little Blue at the Blue Mills, our force then proceeded in a south-west direction, and leaving Independence to the right took a circuitous route for Hickman's Mill, a small place fifteen miles south of Kansas City.

Night had now set in, and the clouded sky betokening a storm soon made the way very dark, augmented by the heavy timber and dense underbrush through which they passed; over rocky cliffs and deep ravines, frequently obliged to proceed in single file for miles the path not being wide enough to admit more than one passing at a time. It was of course an unpleasant ride and necessarily very slow and tedious, and notwithstanding the way was led by a guide who was familiar with the country through which they passed on more than one occasion they were obliged to halt and retrace their steps for a considerable distance.

It was near midnight when the command reached Hickman's Mill and went into camp until morning, when they retraced their course to Independence to join Colonel Ford, who had proceeded to that place the evening previous. Our troops had a great deal of amusement very often at the expense of the bushwhackers; although, it was at the same time very risky and dangerous; they would dress up in butternut and play bushwhacker themselves, and thus find out their camps and places of resort and other secrets. Among the number of schemes about the most laughable was the following: a squadron composed of Companies F and E had cleared out at Camden Point about one hundred and sixty of Thornton's guerrillas; the next morning Captain Bill Green, dressed up in the copper-coloured garb and riding a mile or two in advance of the command, made a grand rush up to the house of a notorious *secesh*, who had the evening before shown them a stock of certificates of loyalty thus hoping to deceive them; but Captain Green was not to be duped, he informed the old gent that the Federals were close by and his horse was played.

Thereupon the old man bustled round gave the captain a fine horse from the stable worth three hundred dollars and bade him "God speed" to Thornton's camp, telling him where it was. But in a few minutes the old man found out his mistake, when he saw the command ride up with Colonel Ford at its head and Captain Green beside him on his fine black charger, he did not show his certificates this time, but he did contribute three more fine horses to Uncle Sam, which he probably got paid for after proving his loyalty.

On the fifteenth of October, General Curtis passed through Kansas City, to Independence, and the next day proceeded to Hickman's Mill, where troops were concentrating, preparatory to the reception of Price's forces. Major Smith, with a portion of the Second Colorado, proceeded to Lexington, a distance of forty miles, where he arrived just after the town had been vacated by a band of bushwhackers, who had charged into the town killing some of the citizens and firing into a boat that was passing up the river; having no other effect than the piercing of her sides and pilot-house with balls, without injury to any of her passengers.

The most extravagant evidences of joy were manifested by the Union citizens of the place on the arrival of our troops. The bandits had been very abusive in their conduct while there, helping themselves to whatever they wanted, loudly denouncing Unionists, and threatening to burn the town; and their departure and the arrival of our troops caused general rejoicing; and everyone was eager to attend to the wants of our men, bringing water and eatables, to satisfy their thirst and hunger. After scouring the country thoroughly and gaining no definite information concerning the movement of the rebel army, the major and command returned to Independence.

On the same day General Curtis received official information of the capture by the rebels of Sedalia and Dresden, towns situated on the Pacific Railroad, and about one hundred miles east of Kansas City, and garrisoned by a small force; also, that Price's entire force, now swelled to twenty-eight thousand strong was steadily marching in the direction of Kansas City. On the twenty-seventh, a reconnoitring column consisting of about eleven hundred cavalry under General Blunt, left Hickman's Mill and proceeded on the road to Lexington, with the determination of striking the enemy before returning if to be found in that part of the country.

Having reached and passed through Lexington, on the afternoon of the nineteenth, General Blunt's advance and Price's vanguard met about ten miles south-west of that place, and a skirmish ensued, during which the enemy endeavoured to surround Blunt's command, by throwing forward two columns, one on the right and the other on the left, while his centre engaged our forces, to cover the movements of his flanking columns.

General Blunt was on the alert and discovered the movement in time to thwart the design of the enemy and ordered our troops to fall back, which they did in time to cut their way out with the assistance of four small howitzers, commanded by Colonel Moonlight, sustaining little or no loss on our part. The guns were planted in a commanding position and their fire directed by Colonel Moonlight in person, and the grape and canister was poured into the enemy's flanks on the right and left having the effect to check their advance until our forces were again formed into line.

General Blunt being satisfied that the enemy was there in strong force gradually fell back, with two companies of the Eleventh and one of the Fifteenth Kansas Cavalry and the artillery under command of Moonlight to protect their rear and cover their retreat. In this manner our troops fell slowly back, sharply contesting the confident advances of the enemy, for about ten miles distance west of Lexington; when night setting in the enemy checked up, but a constant skirmish firing was kept up during the entire night and the next day, until our forces were within ten miles of the Little Blue, when the rebel army halted; while our forces retreated to the Little Blue and, halting, lay upon its east bank until evening, when the entire command crossed.

Colonel Moonlight with the Eleventh Kansas and the artillery was posted on the west bank to defend the crossing, with orders, if necessary, to burn the bridge, for which purpose a torch made from the dry plank was prepared and placed upon the centre of the bridge ready for the match. General Blunt with the principal part of his force proceeded to Independence, eight miles west of the crossing. At eight o'clock on the morning of the twenty-first the enemy made their appearance on the east bank of the creek and immediately commenced an attack on our little force, who gallantly disputed their passage to the bridge, finally applying the torch. It was soon wrapped in flames, which served to check their impetuous advance for a short time.

In the meantime Colonel Moonlight dispatched a messenger to General Blunt, at Independence, informing him of the attack by the rebels and that he would be compelled to fall back and allow the enemy to cross unless reinforced without delay. General Curtis had just completed the organization of the different brigades as the messenger rode into Independence with the dispatch.

The bugle was immediately sounded and the First Division, consisting of the Second Colorado Cavalry (also including the Fifteenth, Sixteenth and Eleventh Kansas Cavalry, the latter already at the scene of action), three companies of the Third Wisconsin Cavalry, and the First Colorado Battery; in all about fifteen hundred men, under the command of Major General James G. Blunt, proceeded to the front at about eleven o'clock in the morning.

The First Brigade, consisting of the Second Colorado Cavalry (Major J. Nelson Smith), the First Colorado Battery (Captain W. D. McLain), and four companies of the Sixteenth Kansas Cavalry, was commanded by our gallant Colonel, James H. Ford.

The column moved forward at a gallop until within one mile of the Little Blue. Here they were joined by Colonel Moonlight, who had been contesting the enemy's advance at the same time slowly falling back; the enemy having succeeded in effecting a crossing both above and below the bridge. To dismount and throw down some rail fences was but the work of a moment, and a line was formed, the Second Colorado Cavalry on the right, the Fifteenth Kansas on the left, and the Sixteenth Kansas in the centre; the battalion of the Third Wisconsin joining Colonel Moonlight.

Moving forward to the right through the heavy timber for the distance of half a mile, our line gained an advanced position, and the Second Colorado was dismounted and in less than half a minute were hotly engaged with the enemy. Pushing forward to the brow of the next hill, a strong force was discovered posted behind a stone wall on a hill to our left, who immediately opened a brisk fire on our advancing column, who faltered not, but returning shot for shot, and steadily advancing succeeded in driving them from the wall, at the same time exposing our own force to a deadly fire from the hill on the left; but our gallant little force succeeded in driving them from their position and forcing them to fall back about one mile.

Advancing to the brow of a hill, our troops had barely time to take up an advantageous position behind a high fence, when a heavy column of the enemy, led by the notorious bushwhacker Todd, who had been promoted to the position of colonel in the rebel army, and who declared he would annihilate the Second Colorado in revenge for the death of many of his followers and several narrow escapes of himself at their hands while he was engaged in bushwhacking in the counties of Jackson and Lafayette.

Our regiment, however, being advantageously posted, poured such a deadly fire into their ranks as to check their advance; and twice they were compelled to fall back, but being strongly reinforced and led by the daring Todd, they came up the third time and our little force was obliged to abandon the position and retire, which they did in perfect good order keeping up a continuous fire upon the advancing foe.

At this period of the engagement, Major J. Nelson Smith, who, by his kind treatment and manly bearing toward both officers and men had won the love and esteem of the entire regiment, while bravely cheering his men and encouraging them to repel the fierce onset of the vastly outnumbering foe, not hesitating to expose his person wherever his presence was necessary, while thus nobly doing his duty he was struck by a minie ball that pierced his left lung and falling from his horse he never spoke again. No truer or braver man ever drew the breath of life.

He fell, as only a hero falls
Facing a deadly foe—
The blood gush'd from the manly heart,
And bathed the palid brow.

One moment gazed that gallant band,
Upon the stricken, there;
Then, one long hoarse determin'd shout
Rose on the burdened air.

One shout—he's dead—revenge! revenge!
A thousand bullets sped,
And hurtling through the rebel band,
Laid many a traitor dead.

Dead! and they laid a mingled mass
Together, man and horse:
Yet, on they came, their legions trod
O'er many a mangled corpse.

But they were met by hands as firm
As e'er a sabre drew:
Unflinching was their Iron front—
They many a rebel slew,

He sleeps—that gallant soldier sleeps,
Within an honoured grave:
Laid there by loving hands, and mourn'd

By many a gallant brave.
Mourned as only soldiers mourn
A hero loved and lost:
Oh! would he were the only one
This cruel war had cost!

At the announcement of his death the men, who almost worshipped him, sent up a savage yell of revenge, and under the command of the brave Captain Green, the next officer in charge, they stood there almost entirely unsheltered and delivered volley after volley that sent a storm of leaden hail into the enemy's ranks, causing many of them to bite the dust, among whom was the notorious Todd, who was pierced by several balls and fell dead from his horse. But the enemy pressed on and our troops were ordered to fall back to their horses. Having mounted, a retreat was ordered and the entire command moved forward on the road to Independence, a distance of eight miles; the retreat being covered by Ford's Brigade.

This gallant band—a mere handful of men in comparison to the overwhelming number of the enemy—under their able and gallant commander sternly contested the enemy's impetuous advance and repelled the frequent fierce charges made by the foe, who were conscious of their vast superiority in point of numbers and stung at the successful resistance made by our troops. Inch by inch was the entire road to Independence sternly and bravely contested by our little force, protecting the rear and holding the impetuous enemy in check, allowing a safe and perfectly orderly retreat of our entire force. Independence was reached at sundown and our troops moved on to the Big Blue, about five miles west of Independence on the Kansas City road, and the day's battle was over.

Here camp was formed, and dismounting from their somewhat jaded horses the men flung themselves upon the ground and were soon sound asleep, with the exception of the picket-guard, who were stationed on the road and kept a vigilant watch upon the enemy's movements who occupied the town during the night. Never was rest and sleep more welcome to our tired forces, having been almost constantly on the alert for the preceding week, scouring the country in every direction, sometimes night and day; and that day, having been hotly engaged with the enemy from nine o'clock in the morning until the evening, it required no effort on their part to soon forget the stirring scenes of the day in a sound slumber.

During the day our wounded were removed from the scene of action to Independence, where the utmost care and attention of the citizens, especially the female portion, was bestowed on them; and be it said to their credit, a considerable number of rebel ladies who resided in the place came to the rescue with bandages and lint to stay the flow of blood and bind up the shattered limbs of our wounded.

But the kind, assiduous attentions of the few Union ladies, of that place was more fully appreciated by our men. Constant in their efforts to ease the sufferers, nothing that in reason could be done was left undone by them in their generous sisterly care of those who suffered and bled for the Union and the old Flag; long will they be held in grateful remembrance by the Second Colorado. Nor less noble, nor less faithfully did our surgeons perform their unpleasant duty of binding up and stitching the ghastly wounds and amputating the fractured limbs of our brave, unmurmuring soldiers; great credit is due them for their constant and untiring energies, exerted to alleviate pain and animate the men with kind words of encouragement and cheerfulness.

The men sustained their injuries with heroic fortitude. One instance deserves particular mention, a young man named Frank Gould, who had but recently been honourably discharged and subsequently was an officer in the Home Guards of Kansas City, at the approach of Price's army, declared his preference to go into battle with his old comrades of the Second, and did so, and was engaged in carrying dispatches on the field when he was struck by a portion of a shell that almost literally tore his shoulder away, he was placed in an ambulance, and taken to Independence; on arriving there, he raised his hat with his remaining arm and feebly swinging it in the air, shouted, "Hurrah for the Second Colorado and the Old Flag!"

The poor fellow lived some time afterward, but finally died, admired and beloved by all who knew him. Just previous to the occupation of the town by the enemy's forces, all of our wounded who could be removed were taken to Kansas City, Major Smith's body was also brought in that night and the entire place was filled with gloom and sadness to see that in a few short hours some of the bravest and best beloved of our regiment had given their hearts blood for the Union cause and the end was not yet; how many more were to be missed from that brave band only time could tell.

CHAPTER 8

The Surrender of General Marmaduke

The day previous to the Battle of the "Little Blue," Captain George West, with about fifty men of his squadron (Company F), was sent from Independence with dispatches from General Curtis to General Blunt, then at Lexington. Upon nearing the latter place he was met by Captain Jack Curtis, who, with two squadrons of the Fifteenth Kansas, had just cut his way out from the enemy that had well nigh surrounded a portion of our forces. Learning from Curtis that General Blunt was falling back on another road, Captain West wheeled about and directing his course across the country found the general, delivered the dispatches and returned to Independence the same night, having ridden over eighty miles without once dismounting.

The captain humorously remarked that, "General Price had reason to congratulate himself upon the fact that I met Curtis as I did; otherwise he would have been whipped then and there, or else—I should; although many would have had serious doubts about my being able to cope with 'Old Pap,' who was said to have largely outnumbered me—say, in the ratio of thirty thousand to fifty men."

The day after the battle little was done by either of the forces, aside from manoeuvring, skirmishing and placing troops in position; on our part to guard the fords on the Big Blue, which the enemy would necessarily be obliged to cross in his onward march.

The ford on the road leading to Kansas City was protected by Captain McLain's (First Colorado) Battery and a body of about five thousand troops.

The ford a few miles south—known as Byron's Ford—was not strongly guarded, only a small force being stationed at that point; insufficient to seriously retard the progress of the enemy, who had planted a masked battery of three brass pieces to protect his crossing, which was discovered by Captain Hollaway while deploying his squadron (Company L) as skirmishers.

In the afternoon a party of the enemy were discovered attempting to cross and were fired upon by a portion of the Kansas Militia, when in compliance with orders from Captain Green, commanding the regiment, Captain Holloway with his squadron made a dashing charge, resulting in the capture of one captain, one surgeon, one lieutenant and two privates.

In the evening and during the night the enemy crossed his entire force, his movements accelerated by the fact of General Pleasanton pressing close on his rear with a strong force of cavalry; the enemy's rear guard had scarcely left Independence before Pleasanton's advance entered the town.

Price's army was drawn up in battle order near Westport, three miles south of Kansas City, opposed by Colonel Ford's Brigade, Captain McLain's Battery, and a portion of the Kansas troops, the Kansas Militia having ingloriously fallen back beyond the Kaw River, crossing at Wyandotte.

A political strife was at its height in Kansas at the time of the invasion of Price's army, and unfortunately for the reputation of the people and the State, the spirit of jealousy and contention was carried with them when they arose as one man and marched to the border to repel the enemy's threatened invasion.

No grander sight was ever contemplated than the simultaneous uprising of the citizens of Southern Kansas, when the call was made to take up arms against the invaders. All work was suspended, business houses closed and the people, realizing the exigency of the moment, forgot all else in the determination to defend their homes. Hastily forming themselves into organized companies and regiments, with little or no time to drill or perfect themselves in the arts of war, they marched to the border to await the coming of the foe.

But intriguing parties seeking office, embraced the opportunity to urge their selfish claims upon the people, and, what with intriguing and wire-pulling, soon excited a feeling of disgust and dissatisfaction in the ranks, having a tendency to destroy confidence and obliterate all feelings of patriotism; many were under the impression that the foe was not advancing, but the campaign was gotten up for speculation among leading politicians; consequently they became disheartened and thousands of them stacked their arms and refused to cross the State line. Only a minor proportion of the large number who started for the scene of action ever saw the face of the enemy by their action very forcibly bringing to mind the couplet:

The King of France, with ten thousand men.
Marched up the hill and down again!

One regiment of infantry from Jefferson County, that reached Olathe four hundred and eighty strong, came into Kansas City the day previous to the Battle of Westport led by their colonel with only ninety men, the balance having absolutely refused to proceed any further; a good many of their officers finding they could not induce the men to move forward threw away their swords and taking up muskets in their stead bravely joined the ranks, and with the heroic little band followed their gallant leader to meet the foe. Early in the morning of the twenty-third of October, the battle of Westport began.

General Pleasanton came up with and engaged the rear of the enemy. At the commencement of the fight, General Brown came to Pleasanton and reported his skirmishers driven in: "Well," responded the general, "seeing such is the case, what do you intend doing?"

"I don't know, sir!" was the reply.

"Then go to the rear immediately and consider yourself

under arrest;" was the stern command of General Pleasanton, highly incensed that an officer should exhibit such ignorance or cowardice in the presence of the enemy. Some sharp artillery practice ensued, in which Captain McLain's First Colorado Battery, consisting of three-inch rifled parrotts, and supported by a portion of the Second Colorado Cavalry, commanded by Captain Boyd, did great execution in thinning the ranks of the enemy—the guns capable of throwing shell three miles with precision.

A desperate charge was made by the enemy, for the purpose of capturing a portion of this battery that was particularly annoying to them; but they were handsomely repulsed, with heavy loss in killed and wounded and prisoners on their part. The lane up which they charged was literally strewn with dead and wounded men and horses. The battle ground extended over a large area and at different points, the fight raged with greater or less fury for several hours, when the enemy was discovered moving off his large train and by three o'clock in the afternoon the entire rebel army was in full retreat toward the Arkansas River.

Our forces immediately engaged in the pursuit, a column under Colonel Moonlight bearing off toward Olathe, while the main force followed in the rear. A column consisting of the Second Colorado and the Sixteenth Kansas Cavalry, under Colonel Jenninson, pushed forward and succeeded in over taking and suddenly striking the enemy on his right flank, six miles southeast of Little Santa Fe and fifteen miles from Westport. Considerable consternation was exhibited by the rebels, who supposed that our entire army was upon them. Hastily forming two lines of battle, consisting of about six thousand men, and placing a battery in position, they greeted us with several rounds of shot and shell, which, fortunately for us, had no other effect than to cause the bobbing of several heads belonging to persons who had never been under fire and on this occasion thought it policy to be polite even to the enemy.

Having no artillery and our force being insufficient to contend with the enemy, we were compelled to fall back a distance of three miles, where we bivouacked for the night.

Incidents were not wanting to show the spirit of cool courage and determination of our men during the engagement with the enemy. Private James Ross, of Company E, Second Colorado Cavalry, had taken three prisoners and was conducting them to the rear, when one wheeled his horse about and attempted to escape. Ross turned in his saddle to shoot him, when he himself received his death wound from a musket ball; notwithstanding, he succeeded in safely bringing in the other two prisoners, turned over his arms to his company commander and lived until the next day.

Private Iker, of the same company and regiment, during the fight had used all his carbine cartridges and discharged the contents of both of his revolvers, when clubbing his carbine he dashed up to a rebel and struck him dead from his horse and immediately fell dead himself pierced by a rebel ball.

By sunrise on the morning of the twenty-fourth, the entire division, under Generals Curtis, Pleasanton and Blunt, moved forward in pursuit of the retreating rebels, who were a considerable distance in the advance and making strenuous exertions to increase that distance, only anxious to be "let alone" that they might make good their escape from what they were now fully persuaded was a precarious situation. Their booty in the way of subsistence, of which they expected to get abundance in the country through which they passed, proved altogether insufficient in quantity to fully supply the demands of so large a force, which had constantly been augmenting since their arrival on Missouri soil; and in order to avoid the disastrous consequences of being reduced to actual starvation in the end, they were obliged to subsist on less than half rations, together with what scanty supplies could be foraged in the sparsely settled country through which they were obliged to pass.

The rebel general, Sterling Price, by his former manoeuvres had won the deserved reputation of being a skilful, cunning and able leader—in truth, the "most daring and successful raider that the Confederate army could boast of." Ever on the alert and aware of the danger of delay, he caused the retreat to be conducted with as much rapidity as the circumstances would permit, allowing no more time to halt than was absolutely necessary to rest his already weary and hard-pressed followers. Our forces eagerly joined in the pursuit, which was continued until after night had set in, marching the distance of forty miles, before bivouacking on the north side of the Marias des Cygnes, a large creek on whose south bank the next day's battle was fought that proved so disastrous to the rebels.

The night was very dark, the sky overclouded and at midnight a cold, chilling rain began to fall, making it very disagreeable and unpleasant, although not enough to arouse our men from the sound and refreshing slumber they were enjoying; having, as soon as the halt was ordered, laid themselves down with the ground for a bed, their saddles for a pillow and a blanket for a cover.

During the night the enemy's pickets had been discovered and the whereabouts of the rebel force ascertained; and, at two o'clock in the morning, a portion of the Second Colorado on the left and the Fourth Iowa on the right, moved forward as skirmishers to dislodge the enemy from the brow of the hill of which they had taken possession. In the early part of the night, Companies E, I and K, of the Second, under the command of Captain Kingsbury, had been reconnoitring in the advance and under cover of the darkness of the night, suddenly came upon the rebel pickets and succeeded in killing six of them and wounding several. Forming in line, the battalion awaited reinforcements before moving forward, and in the meantime Captain Kingsbury dispatched, at different intervals, four messengers back to the commanding general informing him that the enemy were near and in force.

After awaiting nearby two hours, Captain Hinton rode up and informed Kingsbury that Blunt's Division, which had been in the advance of the column the preceding day, had been ordered to halt, to allow Pleasanton's Division to take the advance, and, in consequence of the necessary delay, the column was five or six miles back. Upon the strength of this information, Captain Kingsbury, realizing the imprudence of attempting to hold the line unsupported, faced the battalion about and fell back a considerable distance, when they were met by the Eighth Missouri, who, owing to the change in the divisions, mistook our men for the rebels, supposing themselves to be in advance of the column.

The order to unsling carbines was given and the rattle of arms was distinctly heard by Kingsbury's Battalion when the captain halted the command and riding for ward alone, succeeded after some time in impressing the incredulous colonel of the Eighth, with the true nature of the circumstances and the identity of our force; and equally as difficult was it to convince him of the fact that the pickets had been driven in and the whereabouts of the enemy's advance line; in order to satisfy his inquisitiveness and incredulity, Captain Kingsbury ordered his orderly-sergeant, Ferree, to take four men and approach near enough to draw the fire of the enemy and at the same time not expose themselves unnecessarily. Ferree approached the out posts and was hailed by a sentinel: "Who goes there " which question was answered, Yankee-like, by Ferree's response: "Who are you?"

"Confederate soldiers," was the reply and the sound of his voice had scarcely died away when the vivid flash and sharp report of the carbines of the brave sergeant and his daring comrades drew upon them the concentrated fire of a number of the enemy, causing quite a shower of leaden hail to fall around our boys, who having obeyed orders and accomplished the desired object, retired and joined their command, the colonel having expressed himself fully satisfied that if he had been doubtful all was removed as it was certain there was an enemy in the front.

Resuming his march to the rear in order to regain the regiment, Captain Kingsbury was met by Major Hunt of General Curtiss' staff, with orders to proceed to the front and in connection with the Eighth Missouri and Second Arkansas in the centre, the Fourth Iowa on the right and the Colorado Battalion on the left, to advance upon the enemy's line and open the ball, which order was promptly obeyed just before daybreak, and notwithstanding the fall of a cold rain and the darkness of the night our troops silently advanced amid a shower of musket-balls from the enemy, the flash of their guns distinctly visible at every discharge.

It was the hour just before day, which is said to be the darkest—which assertion was literally true in the present instance—the darkness, increased by overclouded sky and the pouring rain, rendered it so great that it was with difficulty that our line was discernible at the distance of a few paces; the rebels aware of our coming by the tramp of our horses, kept up a continuous line of fire from their carbines, aimed at random, which accounted for the slight execution done.

It was a grand and somewhat exciting scene—our line steadily advancing to drive the rebels and gain possession of the hill on which they were posted; their presence made known only by the vivid and incessant flash and sharp, ringing report of their rifles; the constant whirring sound of the little leaden messengers of death that fell around them resembling in sound the sudden rushing of a bee past one's ear, although not so pleasant to a nervous person made sensibly aware of the dangerous mission of the former. In the meantime day began to break in the east, dimly discovering the position of the enemy, and simultaneously with its dawn the deep welcome thunder tones of our cannon, planted two miles in the rear, broke upon our ears, and presently the whizzing, whirring, howling shell came rushing over our heads, and falling rather short of its mark exploded in rather un comfortably close proximity to our line, having the effect to make our men feel nervous and anxious as to their own safety; the experienced gunners discovered their shortcomings and elevating their pieces the next shells burst directly among the enemy, creating considerable consternation in their ranks and causing great confusion, when they broke and fled over the brow of the hill pursued by our eager and exult ant forces, who made the welkin ring with their prolonged shouts and cheering hurras.

The hill gained by our forces, the rebels were discovered drawn up in line, about three thousand strong, three hundred yards on the other side, awaiting our appearance. Placing a battery of two guns in position, they saluted our troops with a few rounds of shot and shell and breaking ranks crossed the Marias des Cygnes at the ford, when General Sanborn was heard to say, "Send out that Colorado Battalion to clear the ford, they'll fight."

Upon receiving the order, Captain Kingsbury's Battalion of the Second Colorado, charged and carried the ford without loss, very unceremoniously interrupting the strenuous efforts of the enemy to blockade the crossing by felling trees into it, for the purpose of delaying our advance. The trees were soon removed and Sanborn's Brigade crossed over and found the enemy drawn up in line a few hundred yards in advance, with a battery of two guns in position.

Instantly forming line of battle, with the Eighth Missouri on the left, the Second Arkansas on the right, and the Colorado Battalion, under Kingsbury, in the centre; our advance moved forward out of the woods, along and on both sides of the road, when the enemy opened his battery and throwing a few shells in the ranks of the Eighth Missouri, they hastily fell back under cover of the woods, and a few well-directed shots had the same effect upon the Second Arkansas, leaving the Colorado Battalion alone and still advancing under a galling fire from the battery, the enemy expecting that a similar experiment with it would be productive of a similar result. Captain Kingsbury said his orders were to advance and he intended to obey them, although he was positively forbidden to charge the enemy. Presently the rebel line gave way and hauling off their battery left our forces masters of the field.

At this juncture Major Hunt rode up, and remarking to Kingsbury that his Battalion had done sufficient for that day, ordered him to halt and rejoin his regiment when it came up. The battalion was dismounted and the horses fed from an adjacent cornfield, while the advance of the command pushed on in pursuit of the retreating army. At five miles distance from the crossing of the Marias des Cygnes, the enemy again formed line of battle to contest the impetuous advance of our troops; a sharp skirmish fight lasted for a few minutes, when Colonel Benteen's Brigade made a brilliant charge, resulting in the capture of Generals Marmaduke and Cobbell, five hundred other prisoners and six pieces of cannon.

The rebels fought well, and their resistance was determined, but they were not prepared to withstand nor repel a charge from our forces, being armed only with carbines or rifles, while a great portion of our men were armed with sabres and revolvers, and one regiment, the Fourth Iowa Cavalry, carried Spencer's Carbines, a seven-shooter, and considered a very effective weapon.

The charge and capture occupied but a few minutes, the enemy convinced of the uselessness of resistance to the confident and determined onset of our forces.

Had the suggestions of General Blunt been followed, the result would doubtless have been the capture of a large portion if not the entire rebel army. His plan was to continue the pursuit that morning with the main body, but to throw a strong force across the Marias des Cygnes, at a ford three miles above and to the right, and strike the rebels on their right flank and thereby cutting their army in two, when the rear portion, being completely surrounded, would have been compelled to surrender at discretion, and it would have required no strenuous exertion on our part to have succeeded in capturing the remainder of the already discouraged and dispirited enemy. And the long, tedious and expensive pursuit would have been avoided; but his plan was not adopted, and hence the result.

After the battle which was on the prairie, the ground was strewn with the dead and wounded; particularly at the crossing of Mine Creek, a small stream near the scene of the charge, where the rebels were closely pursued by our men, while in their hurried attempts to cross over and escape many threw away their guns without attempting to discharge them, so great was their desire to escape being taken prisoners; although those who fell into our hands seemed well satisfied with the exchange effected, and some of them were disposed to be jocular over the event, indulging in humorous allusions to their condition; to the inquiry as to where he belonged, one of them replied: "To the whipped Confederacy." Another, to the same inquiry, said he was "One of Price's 'purps!'"

During the charge, a private soldier rode to General Marmaduke with an imperative demand for his surrender; disdaining to become the prisoner of one so far beneath his rank. Marmaduke demurred haughtily against complying, saying something about his not being the proper person to surrender to, when the cavalry man's carbine was quickly brought to a level with his eye, and the "Duke" was glad to acknowledge its power, and submitted to be taken captive, by "a private," without another murmur, glad to have escaped a worse fate. The youthful soldier who captured him was rewarded for his bravery by being presented with Marmaduke's belt and revolvers, by General Curtis.

The rebel general was a large man, of stout muscular form and rather portly; he wore a light jeans coat and pants of the same material, and altogether his general appearance and style of dress was calculated to impress one with the idea that an old Pennsylvania farmer stood before him, instead of the shrewd, cunning and able officer that he had proved himself to be on more than one occasion.

Sterling Price considered him as the most able and responsible officer of his command, and hence entrusted to him the protection of the rear of the rebel army and holding in check the pursuing forces. Another stand was made by the enemy at Little Osage, a small stream of that name, but our forces succeeded in driving them as before, with little or no loss on our side.

Almost destitute of rations, our regiment was ordered to proceed to Fort Scott, where they arrived at ten o'clock that night, having ridden sixty miles that day without food and but little rest. The regiment joined in the pursuit almost entirely unprovided with rations, some of the companies having no more than a ration of hard tack; consequently, a large proportion of the men were without food for over thirty hours, during which time they were almost constantly in the saddle. For two hours previously to the arrival of the command at the fort, it was with the greatest difficulty that the men kept their seats in the saddles, on account of having been deprived of sleep for so long a period; requiring constant exertion to maintain an upright position.

So exhausted were they, that on coming into camp at the fort, many of them were able merely to dismount, ungirth the saddle, and laying it down threw themselves beside it and were almost immediately wrapped in a sound slumber. On the morning of the twenty-sixth, the pursuit was resumed, all the men with worn-out horses having been sent back to Kansas City, under command of Captain Evans, of Company A, Second Colorado. The rebels had been too closely pursued to allow them to take Fort Scott, which would have been an easy matter for them to have accomplished had they not been so strongly pressed by our forces in the rear. But their safety was in rapid retreat, and every effort on their part was made to accelerate their movements; a large number of their wagons were burned, ammunition destroyed and arms thrown away; in fact the route of their retreat was literally strewn with abandoned property of every description.

Chapter 9

The Final Pursuit of the Rebel Army

On the twenty-seventh, the army reached Carthage, Missouri, a village that had been partially destroyed with fire by a band of bushwhackers, some five weeks previous.

Here they found the ambulance that contained the medicines belonging to the rebel army almost entirely consumed by fire; together with abandoned arms, horses, saddles and camp equipage; everything indicating a panic in the rebel ranks, and extreme haste in their endeavour to outstrip their pursuers. On the twenty-eighth, the near presence of the foe became distinct.

Therefore Colonel Ford, commanding the brigade, ordered Captain Holloway's Company (L) to proceed as skirmishers, and hard and desperate encounters took place, resulting in the entire routing of Price's army; throwing death and dismay through his whole command. Many deeds of valour and bravery could be recited of the Second Colorado and their brave companions in arms on that eventful campaign: very much is lost to history, as those who were witness rest in their graves.

Private Karr, of Company H, whose horse, in the battle, had been shot through the head and was bleeding profusely, when told by his company commander that he had better go to the rear, took a parting fire at the enemy and fell back a few paces, reloading his carbine as he went and when completed wheeled about and rejoining the ranks gave the foe the benefit of "one more round," repeating the act several times, momentarily expecting his horse to fall, but loath to quit the field—coolly remarking that all he wanted was to "give the rascals one more shot."

Private Click, of Company C, who was a considerable distance in the rear when the battle commenced, in charge of a mule team, drove up to the lines, while the guns were thundering away and shot falling thick around him, deliberately stopped and, with the coolness of a man about taking a small contract, shouted, "Halloo, here! what do you want done with this team?" causing considerable merriment along the line where his voice was heard. The remarkable degree of cool courage exhibited by the men, had the effect of daunting the enemy, they not daring to "charge" where the opposing forces were apparently determined to maintain their ground at all hazards.

Particularly did they evince a wholesome dread of the "White Horse Regiment," as they were wont to term the Second Colorado Cavalry; two companies of which, E and K, were mounted upon white chargers. Nor was their fear based upon ground less reasons, for upon several occasions they had suffered greatly under their galling fire, which told severely upon their numbers by thinning their ranks, and whenever the "Second" came into an engagement, the dismayed rebels would remark, "There goes that White Horse Regiment." And well they might so exclaim, for in every perilous place they were to be found; their powers of endurance seemed to exceed all others.

The night succeeding the Battle of Newtonia, a courier arrived from Fort Scott with a telegraphic dispatch from General Rosecranz, containing orders for the immediate abandonment of the pursuit, the disbanding of the army, and the return of the troops to their respective places of rendezvous. Inopportune as the receipt of this order was at the time, General Curtis felt bound to obey its requirements, and the next day the army was disbanded and the various organizations started on the return home. When the dispatch reached Fort Scott, it was evident to the commanding officers that Rosecranz was ignorant of the true state of the campaign and a dispatch was immediately forwarded to Washington in regard to the matter, apprising the authorities of the movements of the two armies and notifying them of General Rosecranz's order.

In reply, a telegram was received from General Grant countermanding Rosecranz's orders, and ordering the pursuit continued until the rebel army were captured or driven across the Arkansas River. The dispatch reached General Curtis the next day, in the evening, he having already marched ten miles from Newtonia on the return.

The command was halted for the night, and on the morning of the thirtieth resumed the pursuit, and arriving at Newtonia the same evening, camped in the town overnight. On the morning of the thirty-first, in accordance with orders from the commanding general, the troops were mustered. The sparse supply of rations on hand—consisting of "hard tack," bacon and coffee, with the addition of a barrel of molasses that the enterprising boys succeeded in "gobbling"—was distributed, and at ten o'clock the remnant of the army, mustering, all told, less than four thousand men, continued the pursuit of the retreating foe in the direction of Fayetteville, Arkansas.

Through an egregious blunder somewhere, the unfaltering band had lost the advantage gained, giving the enemy time to collect their terror-stricken troops, and not only that, but reduced our own force and started them on the return with little or no provision, through a section of country already stripped by the enemy; yet our little army marched twenty-two miles on that day, in a south-east direction, for the purpose of striking the Lexington and Fayetteville Road, which, there was good reason to believe, the enemy had taken with the intention of reaching and crossing the Arkansas River at the nearest practicable point.

Early on the morning of the first of November, the command was visited by a heavy rain that thoroughly soaked their bedding and wearing apparel and roused them from a sound slumber. Just before daylight the rain slackened up and taking advantage of its cessation numerous campfires sprang into existence throughout the encampment, fed by rails from the fences of which the men were not sparing, in their efforts to dry their clothes and warm their thoroughly chilled and benumbed bodies.

By the time that day had fully made its appearance, the brisk fires and the double rations of corn essence that was ordered to be issued had the effect of dispelling the chilly sensations and ere long general good humour prevailed; each one in his turn laughingly relating the mishaps that befell him during the night. How refreshingly they were slumbering, and how the water came down upon them from the hillside and damming up against their bodies, the thick blankets and great-coat repelling and holding it at bay for a time, but how it eventually found its way through completely saturating the bed and deluging the already chilled body with an almost icy bath, causing the recipient to very suddenly assume an upright attitude to avoid an embrace so unrefreshing, while the lips would shape the exclamations they uttered into anything but a prayer.

When the rest had given in their experience, our colonel of the "Second," who had during the entire campaign shared in the danger, toils and privations with the common soldier—eating the same fare and contenting himself with the camp-life, rough as it was came up and good-humouredly remarked: "Well boys, I suppose you are all wet through, so am I. I spread my blankets down between the corn-rows, with my overcoat for a pillow, and being consider ably fatigued was soon in a sound sleep, from which I did not awake until a few minutes ago, my blanket serving to keep the rain off effectually.

"I was congratulating myself upon my comfortable quarters, when raising my head to look about me my pillow, which served as a dam for about fifty gallons of water which had collected above me, suddenly gave way and the entire flood most unceremoniously deluged myself and bed rendering my quarters so uncomfortable that I determined to abandon the spot, which I instantly did, viewing the action in the light of a military necessity; but, boys," continued the colonel, drying himself by the fire and still shivering from the effects of his cold bath, "I'm as wet as a drowned rat!"

The boys had a hearty laugh at the colonel's mishap, which

was as heartily joined in by the colonel himself, who could always relish a joke even though at his own expense. At eight o'clock the army moved forward and in the afternoon reached the Lexington and Fayetteville road, and went into camp three miles from the scene of the memorable Battle of the "Pea Ridge," having marched fifteen miles through the rain and mud. The ground was now thoroughly soaked and the water lay in pools, rendering it difficult for the men to obtain a spot on which to rest comfortably for the long, dreary night.

Rain fell for the greater part of the night and the entire following day; the command remaining in camp awaiting its cessation. The brigade, under Colonel Benteen, that was some distance in the rear, arrived during the afternoon, together with the ambulance-train that had not been with the command since the charge at Marias des Cygnes.

Another disagreeable night was passed by the troops, who resorted to all sorts of expedients to remedy their unpleasant situation, rendered more so by the great scarcity of provisions in camp and the almost barren prospect of soon obtaining a supply adequate to the requirements of so large a number in the country through which we passed; the rebel army having stripped the inhabitants on their line of retreat of almost everything that was eatable, with the exception of beef, of which a plentiful supply was obtained and heartily partaken off by the men; with the scant allowance of hard bread on hand, a meal was prepared that was eaten with a keen relish, to appease appetites that were sharpened by the cold, chilly atmosphere, the falling rain and the fatiguing march.

That night, as the one preceding, it rained almost incessantly, flooding the ground to such an extent as to render it almost impossible to escape the water either from overhead or from beneath. Some of the men who crowded into a few log cabins that were near, fared comparatively well; but many were compelled to remain up the greater part of the night; others making a foundation of rails and sticks of wood, spread their wet blankets upon it and slept as well as could be expected under the circum stances.

On the morning of the third of November, the command again took up the line of march, in spite of the falling rain and muddy road, and at about eight o'clock, we passed over the battle ground of "Pea Ridge," the furrowed ground and the scarred and torn trees giving evidence of the fierce struggle between the Union and the Rebel forces in the year 1861. At ten o'clock it commenced snowing and continued throughout the balance of the day. A march of eighteen miles was accomplished and the army went into camp on the left of the road, among a dense growth of underbrush, which served the double purpose of a barrier to the cold, chilling wind and a partial protection from the storm of snow and sleet.

Abundance of wood was at hand and soon huge fires were built throughout the camp, and the now thoroughly hungry men were soon busy frying, roasting and broiling beef, of which a plentiful supply was obtained on the road and driven into camp. At three o'clock on the morning of the fourth, the camp was aroused by the shrill notes of the bugle sounding the assembly, and in one hour's time, the command was moving forward in the direction of Fayetteville, Arkansas, where a portion of the rebel army, under the notorious Fagan, was laying siege to that post; which was defended by the First Arkansas Infantry regiment, with two small howitzers. The storm had now abated, although it was yet stinging cold, and the command pushed forward as fast as the condition of the roads and the jaded stock would admit of, to relieve the heroic garrison from the attack of five times their number, assisted by two pieces of artillery.

The thunder of the cannon was distinctly heard, and our troops eagerly pushed forward with the almost certain expectation of having an engagement with the enemy; but Fagan had his scouts out, and being made aware of our approach raised the siege and fled in the direction of Cane Hill, where the main body of Price's army was camped. The command reached Fayetteville at eleven o'clock, the rebels having abandoned the siege, three hours' previous. The garrison and the citizens of the town were necessarily frightened at the unexpected appearance of such a large force of the enemy, and were greatly relieved upon witnessing our approach. The siege had lasted some four hours, resulting in the killing of a rebel lieutenant and two privates; the garrison suffering no loss further than the wounding of one man, and the damaging of a few houses with rebel shot and shell.

One conspicuous house, into the cellar of which was congregated fifty or sixty women and children, was completely riddled; five shells having passed directly through it, and one of them exploding in the kitchen shattered the walls in a frightful manner. A solid shot fired at this house, passed through the hewed-log walls and striking a mule killed it instantly. On arriving at the post, the command immediately went into camp and remained during the day to rest the jaded stock. At twelve the next day, they were again in motion, pursuing the route taken by the retreating enemy, through the Ozark Mountains, in a south-west direction toward Cane Hill, a little village nearly twenty miles distant from Fayetteville.

That night our troops camped at Prairie Grove. Here the men feasted on the abundance of apples that were found in the neigh boring orchards, affording a luxury that was altogether unexpected and consequently all the more welcome. These together with plenty of beef, pork and sorghum molasses, that was discovered hidden away, afforded a living that was very heartily partaken off and very highly appreciated by the men.

The ground exhibited abundant evidence of the hardly contested battle fought here in 1862. The prairie, containing some two hundred acres, was entirely surrounded by a grove of small timber, inside of which the Union army was camped, and hundreds of tent stakes were still protruding from the ground; grape-shot, percussion shells and musket balls were strewn about; trees were scarred and torn, and in some instances entirely severed by a passing shot.

On the morning of the sixth, the pursuit was renewed; about noon, the command reached Cane Hill and found it had been evacuated by the rebel forces in the greatest haste and alarm—having been informed by their scouts that a Federal force, thirty thousand strong, was rapidly approaching to capture or annihilate the entire rebel army. On receiving this information, the greatest consternation prevailed and, although it was late in the evening, orders were issued to march immediately; and disencumbering themselves of everything that could cause them any delay, they fled precipitately in the direction of the Arkansas Eiver, in the hope of reaching and crossing it before being over taken.

All of their sick, who were unable to proceed without the aid of ambulances, were left here in charge of one of their surgeons, who fled that morning, telling the poor fellows that he could do nothing for them and that he would be killed if he was captured. The men had been impressed with the same idea, and at the approach of our army, those who were able, left the rude, uncomfortable buildings in which they were placed and took to the woods, some crawling upon their hands and knees. Several of these were found by our men and brought back and supplied with rations and medicine of which they were entirely destitute. Their gratitude for the acts of humanity practiced by our troops was almost without bounds, tears of joy streaming from their eyes, at the unexpected kindness; knowing well the brutality with which our troops were treated in the South by their men, they feared a retaliation on their part of ours if taken by them.

The rebels, dead and wounded, were picked up all along the road and placed in our ambulances to be taken care of.

The rebel army was driven to the line of Texas, when the pursuit was given up and our troops returned back weary and worn; some of their horses dying under them from sheer exhaustion. A portion of several companies of the regiment were detailed to escort General Fisk, who had charge of the prisoners; with orders to take them to the nearest shipping point to be exchanged; this done, the different divisions were marched back to headquarters. For gross mismanagement and short-sightedness, coupled with an extreme degree of audacity and daring, this campaign had few parallels.

Chapter 10

My Farewell to the Regiment

While the rebel army occupied Independence, it was completely surrounded by our forces. On the east, by Pleasanton with nearly sixteen thousand men; on the west, by Generals Curtis and Blunt with a force of at least eight thousand; while on the north, egress was blocked up by the Missouri River; and on the south, by the "Little Blue," whose miry bottom and steep banks rendered it impassable for cavalry and artillery, while the timber and heavy growth of underbush was so dense as to prevent the approach of a body of troops to the streams, except by the roads leading to the fords. General Curtis had the advantage of the strong, natural defence afforded by the "Big Blue," running directly between the Union and Rebel forces, and forming a line of complete breastworks, and which could only be crossed at three points:

At its mouth on the Missouri River, where the stream was hardly fordable and where the timber was so dense that it was rendered difficult of access except by small parties, consequently offering no inducements for the passage of an army; at the ford on the Kansas City and Independence Road, commanded by high bluffs on the west bank where a battery could command the approach to the crossing and sweep the narrow canon through which the road passed on emerging from the stream; and at what was known as "Byron's" Ford, a few miles south and on Curtis' extreme left, and the most practicable passage for the rebel army, and the one through which the rebels would attempt to force their way on discovering the precarious situation in which they were placed by the Union forces aided by the natural barriers to their farther progress; but either through a culpable neglect on the part of the commanding-general, or the lack of proper confidence in his own force and the strength of his position, this point was very lightly guarded, and the rebel army escaped from a position in which to use a correct expression in reference to the matter at the time, they were "completely corralled."

The next blunder was committed at the Marias Des Cygnes, when General Blunt's practicable proposition was unheeded: to cross the stream with a portion of the army, and strike the enemy on his right flank thereby dividing his forces and completely surrounding the rear divisions, compelling their surrender and the consequent surrender of Price's entire army. Another manifest display of bad generalship exhibited itself through the entire campaign: With the exception of but a single instance our army never marched in more than single columns, and varying in length from five to fifteen miles; while the enemy proceeded in from two to four columns abreast and were at all times enabled to present a solid front, well supported, when attacked in the rear by a part of our scattered forces.

The exceptional instance alludes to Colonel Moonlight's Regiment which left the command after the Battle of Westport, and proceeded along the border by way of Olathe, Paola and Fort Scott, rejoining the command at the latter mentioned place. During the charge at Marias Des Cygnes, although on the open prairie, but one division participated, while another halted in the immediate vicinity to feed their horses.

At the Battle of Newtonia only nine hundred of our men were engaged, and they stood there, gallantly and heroically contesting the field against ten times their number for nearly three hours before the next division arrived, although they came up at the gallop on receiving the dispatch announcing the opening of the engagement by Blunt's forces. After going into camp the following general order was issued by the general commanding:

Headquarters, Camp Arkansas, Nov. 8.

The object of this organization and campaign is accomplished. The rebel army under General Sterling Price has been confronted, beaten in several conflicts and pursued and driven over three hundred and fifty miles, from the Missouri to the Arkansas.

This has been the work of fourteen days. Your marches have been incessant, sometimes for days and nights in rain and snow, and generally on short rations gathered from the herds lost by the enemy. Your privations, toil and gallantry deserve the highest commendation, and the success of the campaign in which you have so gloriously participated, most of you from the beginning to the end, must entitle you to the thanks of your Government and the gratitude of the loyal people of your country.

Your losses are considerable, but nothing in comparison with those of the enemy, who admits a loss in killed, wounded and missing of eight or ten thousand.

All of his cannon but two, a large portion of his small arms, his vast wagon-train loaded with spoils and herds of cattle and horses have been left, burned and scattered in the way of your pursuit. But the greatest achievements of this campaign are the driving of a desperate class of vagrant associates of the rebels so far from your homes and the States you defend. Beside this, your stern resistance and close pursuit saved the towns and garrisons of Kansas City, Olathe, Paola, Fort Scott, Fayetteville, Fort Gibson and Fort Smith, and the valuable public stores of these places; besides checking ulterior purposes of slaughter and desolation contemplated by the invasion in Kansas.

But it would tarnish the brilliancy of your achievements to claim this for yourselves alone, without acknowledging with gratitude the share borne in the brunt of the contest by the troops of Missouri, of Iowa, of Wisconsin, and the militia of Kansas, who shared the dangers, and because of their greater numbers especially deserve more of the honours due the conflicts of the twenty-fourth, twenty-fifth and twenty-eight of October. But to you, including the Brigade of Colonel Benteen, who have shared in most of these battles and continued throughout the long, weary pursuit to the dark and turpid waters of the Arkansas, where your guns thundered in the rear of the starving, terrified enemy, must be accorded the special commendation of the Commanding-General and the generous approval of your country.

The special honour due to distinguished comrades in the campaign will be carefully presented by the Commanding-General in his report to Headquarters, at Washington, and to secure the most exact justice to so many deserving commendation, Commanders of divisions, brigades, detachments and staff-officers will make full reports, directed to Headquarters, Fort Leavenworth, at their earliest convenience.

In parting the general tendered his thanks to the officers and soldiers for their generous support and prompt obedience to orders, and to his staff for their unceasing efforts to share the toil, incident to the campaign. The pursuit of Price in 1864, and the battles of Lexington, Little Blue, Big Blue, Westport, Marias Des Cygnes, Osage, Chariot, and Newtonia, will be borne on the banners of regiments who shared in them; and the States of Missouri, Iowa, Kansas, Colorado, Illinois, Indiana, Wisconsin and Arkansas may glory in the achievements of their sons in this short but eventful campaign. By the commanding-general at least the soldiers of Colorado received the credit they deserved; yet in many of the official reports we find but little credit given them for their endurance, especially in their hard campaigns through Mexico.

The Confederate army being driven from the States of Missouri and Kansas, and the haunts of the bushwhackers being broken up, there was no longer work for such a force, and much to the dismay of the citizens of the State where our troops had been staying the Second Colorado was ordered to leave and report at Fort Leavenworth, Kansas.

The State of Missouri during our stay had changed very much in appearance, instead of the fields lying uncultivated as before, our men at every opportunity had helped the feeble men and women, to put their fences in order and get in crops, and the result was a bountiful yield of everything such as they had not gathered in years, hence their sorrow at the removal of our regiment. During the Price raid our quartermaster with the sick and all regimental property, spare horses and such like, had been camped on Cedar Creek, in Kansas, within sound of the fight; scouts coming in every little while to apprize him of how the battle was getting on.

The mules were kept for a number of hours hitched to the wagons expecting every minute to hear the order to forward march; as the enemy outnumbered our forces so much it seemed almost impossible for them to stand their ground, but the God of Battles decided in our favour and we were recalled and with the rest of the regiment concentrated at Kansas City, marching from there to Fort Leavenworth where we were ordered to the field, to await further developments and camped on a bottom near the garrison; the men doing camp and other duties such as was from time to time assigned them; scouting, escorting and such like active service.

It was but a few weeks ere reports kept coming of Indian depredations on the plains, and the result was the Second Colorado was ordered to Fort Riley for the purpose of stopping the Indian trouble and to chastise the guilty ones. Here a difficulty arose. Companies A and B, whose time was virtually up just about the time of the Price raid, did not like the idea of passing another winter on the plains. Some of the men had gone from the States at the first cry of Pike's Peak, and had left their families behind hoping to get some of the golden treasure. The great uprising in the South fired every patriot heart and commending their dear ones to God's mercy, they threw down the miner's tools and marched valiantly at the sound of the drum.

As the war, was prolonged beyond their expectations they

kept on and on hoping for the end that they could soon go to their loved ones; thus time sped on and many of them had been absent for several years; and when the order came for them to go on the plains again it looked like great injustice after such a faithful servitude.

A request was made that they should have their discharge, which was forwarded to Washington, by their commanding officer, Colonel Jas. H. Ford; marching orders meanwhile had been issued to the regiment and the colonel was absent on furlough, therefore Major Pritchard took command and all left Fort Leavenworth together, but orders were sent after the command to the effect that Companies A and B return next day to Fort Leavenworth preparatory to being mustered out, which order was cheerfully obeyed and bidding goodbye to the rest of the regiment the two companies returned to Fort Leavenworth and going into camp again awaited the coming of the pay master, who on the twenty-first day of December, 1864, paid off and discharged from the Army, Companies A and B of the second Colorado, who, bidding farewell to their comrades, myself and children, went on their way with hopeful hearts.

The regiments of Colorado were unlike those of other States; in this way the men who volunteered in that territory had gathered there to the mines from every part of the globe, and in those regiments every State and almost all Nations were represented; therefore, when discharged, they were scattered again to the four winds with small hope of ever being together again.

As here my travels with the regiment ended I must depend on such information as I gained from time to time by letter. The remainder of the regiment went to Fort Riley and as the Indians were very troublesome it was actively employed in trying to hold them in subjection, and where stationed at Fort Riley, Fort Zarah, Fort Ellsworth, Fort Larned, and other camps. In a communication from Fort Larned it reads;

> We have been visited with a storm the most severe I ever witnessed and I shall never see such another. A scout arrived here on Saturday evening and reported a train which

left here on the eighteenth for Fort Riley, with an escort of forty-two men, was attacked by three hundred Indians, when seventy miles out; lost one man killed; private Joseph Fields, of Company F, private Donahue, of Company M, and one man named Cole, belonging to the first Colorado Cavalry, wounded; the former seriously. They all suffered severely from cold; were obliged to burn a portion of the train to keep from freezing. The boys were somewhat scattered at the time of the attack chasing buffalo; the Indians got between them and the main party, and when the rest came up the Indians betook to flight.

Another letter from Larned says:

We have quite a number of sick here and no one to attend them properly. Lost one man of our squadron since coming here, Rosson of Company M.

One from Fort Ellsworth, January twenty-third, reads;

Company L left Fort Riley on the sixteenth and arrived on the nineteenth *ult*. Distance travelled, ninety miles. We shall proceed to erect huts, or 'burrows' in the ground, whichever way is deemed most expedient. If the kind of weather we have been having for three days past continues, underground apartment will suit us best.

Miles Jain, Sergeant of Company I, writes from Fort Scott:

There are four of us here within the walls of the hospital, three of Company L and one of Company I, all severely wounded. We are waiting for fine weather, to rejoin our regiment. I sometimes console myself, that we escape the suffering you endure with the bad weather, but when I think of the hole through my breast I try to think it is all right as it is.

Such was the fortitude with which they were bearing their sufferings, and trying through it all to encourage each other.

From Fort Zarah, February second, one says:

A small party of men were detailed to cut and haul some dry wood from an island in the Arkansas River, about the distance of a mile from the Post. They had been on the Island but a short time before the report of firearms were heard, and much to the surprise of all, one of their number came running toward the wagons, not reaching them, however, before he fell to the ground. But very few of the party were armed, and supposing there were Indians in the vicinity and not knowing their numbers they concluded to hasten to the Post and give the alarm. Lieutenant Coy was immediately sent out with a party of men, and, on arriving at the spot, found Private Dutton, of Company C, Second Colorado Cavalry, severely wounded in several places; the wounded man was removed to the Post hospital, and slight hopes were entertained of his recovery.

It was supposed there was no more than three Indians on the ground as there was no trail to warrant a different opinion. The four squadrons ordered to this Post, composed of C, E, G and K Companies, arrived on Wednesday evening, the twenty-fifth, *ult*. We had a hard time in making the trip. At Salina we encountered a very severe snow storm which continued for one day and night.

The boys as a general thing suffered to a great extent, more especially K Company, who were without tents. The idea of soldiers marching on the plains at this season of the year should never have been entertained, unless actual necessity required it. On arriving here we relieved several companies of the Third Wisconsin Cavalry, who started for Leavenworth next day.

We took possession of their 'quarters' consisting of holes dug in the ground and covered with brush and dirt. There is nothing tasty nor fanciful about them, but they are comfortable. The duty of this Post is very heavy for the amount of men stationed here. We escort the mail-coach from here to the Smoky Crossing, between this Post and Fort Larned, and about twenty-five miles of the road to

Council Grove; also, all Government trains passing by the Post in either direction. The guard details call for four and five men also per day from each Company.

Fort Zarah is situated on Walnut Creek, about one mile above its entrance into the Arkansas River. It is one hundred and thirty miles west of Fort Riley and thirty-five miles east of Fort Larned. The site is a beautiful one and the only objection to be made to it is the scarcity of timber. On the fifteenth of March, the information reaches us of the sick left behind at Fort Leavenworth, thus:

> Private Lowe, of Company K, is on duty at Attache Camp; George Dickerson, of K, is on furlough; Hicks is lame with the rheumatism; W. W. Jones, Company H, is discharged the service on account of sore eyes; Drullard, of H, went home on furlough, re-enlisted, and got a big bounty in a veteran corps in Illinois; A. Lumbert, of Company C, got discharged and is gone home; D. A. Conklin and Alexander Hamilton are at their usual avocation; D. B. Sweep is at the Post Hospital yet.

March the twenty-first, Company H, of the Second, reached Fort Zarah on their way from Fort Ellsworth to Fort Larned, Lieutenant Albert L. Gooding in command; resuming their march next day accompanied by Companies C and G, of the same regiment, under the command of Lieutenants Spencer and Hennion.

A few days later General Ford passed by on his way to Fort Larned, making the trip from Fort Riley to Fort Zarah in about forty-eight hours, a distance of one hundred and sixty-five miles.

Company K received marching orders to go forward to Fort Larned, from which point General Ford, accompanied by one hundred men, proceeded to the Cimmerone Crossing. Thus it was the sabre of the Second Colorado had no chance to rust in its scabbard, after the redskins here as they had been after the bushwhackers before, scarcely could they breathe a sigh of menace ere it was borne on the wings of the wind to the soldiers of the Second Colorado and they were after them pell-mell.

Chapter 11

Indian Attack

In the early part of May, General Ford with a command of about five hundred men and four howitzers, supplying his troops with twenty days' rations, proceeded south of the Arkansas River to a place known as the Salt Plains, where fifteen hundred warriors were reported to be encamped and refused to be peaceable. From that direction they had been for some time sending out their bands to murder and steal. On the twentieth of May, Joseph Kuhn, Company H, of the Second Colorado Cavalry, and Johnson, of the same regiment, left Fort Larned to hunt stray horses. A few miles west of Fort Zarah they were pursued by five Indians. Endeavouring to make their escape Kuhn's horse was shot and fell, leaving Kuhn dismounted and at the mercy of the Indians, and he was killed and scalped by them after discharging two shots from his revolver.

Johnson's horse becoming frightened and unmanageable he was unable to stop him to render assistance, and returned to report as quickly as possible. An ambulance was sent after the body, which was brought in and buried at Fort Zarah. A party went in pursuit of the Indians, but without success. About the same time a party of fifteen Indians attacked a train at Ash Creek, eight miles east of Larned, and drove off all the mules but two and made their escape, although there were twenty infantry along. It was reported the officer in charge would not allow them to fire. General Ford and command arrived at Fort Larned the same evening.

In the early part of May, Corporal John Harper, of Company K, Second Colorado Cavalry, who was wounded in the arm at the battle of Newtonia and subsequently discharged the service, was killed by bushwhackers near Pleasant Hill, Missouri. At last giving his life for the Union cause.

On the twelfth of June, while escorting the U. S. Mail-coach from Cow Creek to Fort Zarah, Lieutenant Jenkins, of the Second, and six men, were attacked about four miles from the former place by about one hundred Indians. Ordering the coach back Lieutenant Jenkins and his little party heroically stood their ground and fought the bloodthirsty savages, who charged up within ten feet, slightly wounding two men belonging to Company G, Seventh Iowa Cavalry; in the fight one Indian and one pony were killed. On the arrival of the coach at Cow Creek, Captain Hammer, of the Seventh Iowa, immediately started with fifty-five men to the scene of action. The Indians had moved in a south-west direction; chase was then given and, although they had two miles the advance, our force succeeded in overtaking them as they were crossing the Arkansas River, killing and wounding at least fifteen Indians.

Leaving a sergeant and twenty men to guard the crossing, the pursuit was continued three miles on the south side of the river, but being unable to overtake them they were obliged to abandon it. About the same time Sergeant Cronk, Company I, Second Colorado Cavalry, with twenty men, while escorting a train, were attacked by nearly one hundred Indians at the Plum Butes, fifteen miles from Fort Zarah, on the Council Grove Road: our men drove the Indians. Patrick Sullivan got separated from the command and was supposed to have been killed. Sergeant Doud, of Company G, Seventh Iowa Cavalry, with twenty men, drove thirty Indians across the Arkansas River.

Lieutenant Hennion, Second Colorado Cavalry, escorting a train with twenty men, on the eleventh of June, was attacked while in corral near Pawnee Rock by over one hundred Indians, but succeeded in dispersing them without loss. On the same day Corporal Hicks and Private Huestis, Company K, of the Second

Colorado, while bearing dispatches from Larned to Riley were ambushed, killed and scalped. The body of Hicks was horribly mutilated, his head, hands and feet being entirely severed.

The messengers for Fort Dodge, on the tenth, were driven back by eleven Indians. On the twelfth, Fort Dodge was attacked by between three and four hundred Indians and all the mules and horses, except eight, were driven off. Three men were wounded and two killed or captured, their bodies were not found. A heavy fog prevented the discovery of the enemy until they were between the pickets and the Fort. William W. Colburn, of Company I, Second Colorado, was struck by lightning and instantly killed on the fifteenth, at Cow Creek, eighteen miles east of Fort Zarah. He was allowing his horse to graze, holding the lariat in his hand at the time of the casualty. The horse was killed at the same instant.

On the eleventh of June, Lieutenant Richard W. Jenkins, Second Colorado Cavalry, with seven men of the Second Colorado and Seventh Iowa Cavalry, while escorting the mail-coach from Cow Creek Station to Fort Zarah, Kansas, when about four miles from the former station, was attacked by more than one hundred Indians, who rushed in upon him from all sides, wounding two of his men with their lances. With his small force Lieutenant Jenkins succeeded in keeping the Indians at bay until the coach returned to Cow Creek Station and reinforcements arrived, with whom Lieutenant Jenkins gave chase to the Indians, following them for twenty miles, crossing the Arkansas River and pursuing them for five miles on the south side.

Two of the Indians were killed when the attack was first made on the coach and fifteen at the crossing of the river, besides a number killed and wounded whom the Indians succeeded in carrying away with them. A large number of ponies were killed or captured, also a large amount of blankets; robes, etc., and the enemy's camp with all its equipage.

Lieutenant Jenkins' entire loss was two men wounded. The names of the men who so valiantly held their ground were as follows: Lieutenant Jenkins' Quartermaster, Sergeant True, Privates Chaffee, Daly and Heycus, Company I, Second Colorado Cavalry, and Cudding, Platte and Coburn, Company G, Seventh Iowa Cavalry. Great credit was due Lieutenant Jenkins and these seven men, who displayed such coolness and bravery when attacked by such unequal odds.

The Indians all the summer were very persistent in their attempts to harass the troops and murder and plunder at every opportunity; sometimes in small bands and then large ones. In the early Spring ineffectual attempts had been made to break up and punish them, but it seemed to quell them only for a short time. Several scouts were made in force for the purpose of coming in contact with them, but the efforts proved unsuccessful for some time in stopping their depredations.

During these scouts the men sometimes suffered severely from cold and the lack of proper food and sufficient quantity of rations, and being compelled to endure fatiguing marches and the inclement weather to which the plains are subject in the Spring season. From the time of their enlistment the Second Colorado had been almost constantly in the field, their duties had been very arduous, and always hardest in the Winter season, and according to the wording and intent of the agreement, under which they entered the service of the United States, they thought themselves held illegally, as the Rebel army had surrendered or been captured almost entirely.

The troops in the east and south were returning home and being mustered out; in numerous instances troops, that had only served a small portion of their term, were discharged as not being considered a necessity, or under any further obligations to the Government as soldiers, the war being ended. These considerations in connection with the fact that they who enlisted under the one hundred dollars bounty act, and had nearly filled their contract by hard service, were still retained, while other troops were receiving three hundred dollars bounty and being discharged the service ere their term was completed, created a dissatisfaction among the men that was augmented by the fruitlessness of their hard campaign against the Indians.

The men, without an exception, believed themselves entitled to their discharge; and numerous contradictory and countermanding orders, by which they were obliged to be governed, engendered the belief in the minds of the men and great dissatisfaction was the result.

The following lines were sent to the regiment at that time by the author:

To the Gallant Second Colorado.
Chafe not, brave boys, though harsh it seems
To keep thine armour on,
When thinking of loved friends and home,
That ye have left so long.

Thy fame—which bears no darkening spot—
Ne'er let it tarnish now!
No overt act commit, to tear
A laurel from thy brow.

Thy honoured dead, thy living brave,
O! sully not their name!
By bright keen blades, thy ready arms
Have won the wreath of fame.

A fame, a fame, which ne'er will die,
Though each brave heart may sleep
Beneath the blooming flowers of earth,
In a cold bed—and deep.

Tire not! with patience bide thy time,
Thy heavy task is o'er;
And thou may'st, by thine own fireside,
Know all is peace once more.

Thy countless acts of gallant worth—
The glorious scars ye wear—
Oh! mar not the escutcheon bright
Ye well may proudly bear.

Aye, proud! for as time leaves its stamp
Upon each war-worn brow;

So will thy valour brighter shine—
More luminous will grow,

Chafe not, for soon thy march will be
Home to the loved and dear;
The trophies of thy hard campaigns,
Thou, too, wilt carry there.

Then bear them yet a little while,
Nor mar thy glories won
THE GALLANT "SECOND" NEVER LEFT
THEIR WORK, TILL FAIRLY DONE.

Some of the officers and men put forth every effort to settle the vexed question and have the regiment mustered out of the service. The matter was represented at Department Headquarters and also reached Washington, and, about the first of May, an Order was promulgated for the discharge of "Cavalrymen whose term of service expired prior to the first of October, 1865."

This had the effect to partially quiet the agitation for the time, but induced dissatisfaction in regard to the exceptions in favour of those whose term of service extended but a few days, in many instances, beyond the period mentioned in the order.

On the twentieth of May, to the deep disappointment and increased unrest of the men the order was countermanded by General Dodge, Department Commander.

Shortly after the Order was re-promulgated, a District mustering rendezvous established at Fort Riley, and the Assistant Commissary of Musters (Captain U. B. Holloway) proceeded to discharge troops in accordance with instructions received; but it was not until the first of September that orders for mustering out the entire regiment were received, and, on the eighth, the regiment left Fort Riley for Leavenworth and was mustered out of service, in which it faithfully and honourably served, on the twenty-third of September, 1865.

Weary, battle-scarred and worn they clasped hands and bade farewell, some never to meet again on earth. The tear drop trembled on the eyelid of many; wounds on the battlefield, days of suffering in the hospital, and hair-breadth escapes, had bound them together as brothers. Although going home to see father, mother, wife or chosen ones, yet a sadness hung over that parting.

Lines Written by the Author, at the Request of Co. "A," on the Death of a Comrade at Fort Craigge, Mexico.

He sleeps; his brow is cold in death,
We've laid his lifeless form to rest,
In grave clothes he is laid away,
The last kind hand his own hath press'd.

He sleeps, and who will bear the news,
The tidings sad, to friends at home,
Or will he sleep forever there,
Unmourned, in that cold lonely tomb.

A stranger in a stranger land,
His kindred, will they never hoar,
How he hath fought, and sickening died
Or how he filled a soldiers bier.

Oh, cruel thought, no father dear,
No mother's kiss upon that brow,
No brother, sister, loved ones near,
And hath he died uncared for now.

Unwept, our comrade tried and true,
Proved in the battles dismal roar,
Ah! no a soldier's heart is kind
As brother's love, they love and more.

Not one dry eye gazed on that tomb,
We loved him he was true and kind,
It cast a shadow o'er the camp,
Each heart in sadness then wil't find.

He sleeps, our brother soldier rests,
The trump of God he next will hear,
And may we answer to that call
And meet our loving comrade there,

Appendix 1

THE SECOND REGIMENT OF COLORADO—
AN INDEPENDENT VIEW

I have endeavoured in writing this history to be impartial, and that my readers may not think I have gone beyond the truth in flattering the Second Regiment, of Colorado, I will add the record as it appeared in *The Conservative*, a paper published in Leavenworth City, in the Fall of 1864, it was headed "A Gallant Regiment" and read thus:

> Amid the many, it seems almost invidious to select the one where all done so well, it seems unjust to make an exemplar of a portion. But every officer and soldier of the Kansas Division of the Army accord the highest meed of praise for all soldierly qualities to the gallant Second Colorado Cavalry, to its able and valiant officers and its capable commander, Colonel James H. Ford. Our citizens were gratified by the appearance of these Veteran Soldiers. Eight companies of the Second Colorado arrived here from Fort Scott and were received by Colonel James H. Ford, Majors Pritchard and Curtis and other gallant gentlemen. They marched through the streets of our city, a pageant more imposing to the thoughtful observer than if, in all the fresh pomp and brightness of the camp or rendezvous, they were starting fresh for the field of duty.
>
> Weapons soiled and battered, garments stained and torn, horses broken down and lean; with their guidons draggled,

rent and stained; not in dishonour, but proudly bringing in their tattered folds the scars of triumphal contest; but, above all, with the proof of valour in the wounded heroes who, in the ambulance train, brought up the rear; all these things gilded the show and aided in making the scene noteworthy. The Second Colorado Cavalry has from the first been in the front and borne the brunt of the fight. We as Kansans will gratefully treasure its name. With our own gallant boys it largely contributed to preserve the State from devastation and to keep unstained its proud record. As Americans we owe it even more.

No body of men deserve a prouder place in the Pantheon which nations rear over its heroes. In its ranks are men from all States, who, isolated among the mountains seeking wealth and carrying civilization with them, at the first gun of the Rebellion sprang to arms, throwing away the golden prize, and musket in hand seeking their country's foe. That brilliant campaign in New Mexico bears the names of a portion of the Second. Under Colonel Ford and Lieutenant-Colonel Dodd (their captains) two companies, A and B, participated in the whole of that vigorous conflict with the Texans. Another portion, under Colonel Dodd, Lieutenant-Colonel Curtis and the lamented Major Smith, constituting what was then known as the Second Colorado Infantry, participated in that other brilliant campaign in the Indian Territory during the summer of 1863.

They were at Cabin Creek and afterwards at Honey Springs, where Captain Green with his command captured the Flag of the Twenty-ninth Texas. They marched to Perryville and after wards occupied Fort Smith, on the thirty-first of August, 1863. The Second and Third Regiments were then consolidated into a Cavalry organization.

Shortly afterward it was placed on duty in Western Missouri, with headquarters at Kansas City. Its history is well known for the past year. Our border has been kept free from marauders by its activity and valour, while the murderous bush whackers have had abundant reason to dread the Second Colorado. Through the past Summer it has had numberless fights and lost many gallant officers and men.

During the Paw Paw Rebellion, Colonel Ford was in command of the pursuing force. At Camden Point and elsewhere the rebel Thornton felt their power.

When the invasion of Price aroused the border to impending danger, the Second Colorado had just been ordered to report to this Department. The Indian War had caused this change. A portion of the regiment was at Fort Leavenworth when, on the eighteenth *ult.*, the proclamation of martial law was prepared. It took the field immediately, and for some days before General Blunt moved toward Lexington, Colonel Ford, from In dependence, was scouring the country thoroughly. Major Smith entered and left Lexington the day before General Blunt's reconnoitring column. From the commencement of the campaign to the wearying homeward march at its triumphant close, the history of the Second Colorado is written in light. In every fight, battle and skirmish the regiment, or some portion thereof, has been engaged.

At Little Blue, where fell the gallant Smith, to the stormy three hours, at Newtonia, they have borne themselves patiently and heroically, like the gallant soldiers and true patriots they are. On the Big Blue, Captain Green with his famous gray-horse squadron was engaged with a body of rebel cavalry that had taken the main Kansas City Road instead of the one at Byron's Ford, by which our position was flanked. It was Captain Green, with the Second Colorado, who opened the ball on Sunday morning at Westport—a day ever memorable to Kansas, as its glorious results saved our State.

At the Trading Post its gray-horse squadron with one other

(the Battalion under Captain Kingsbury) as the advance, fired the last shot on the evening of the twenty-fourth, and the first one which, long before dawn, welcomed in that victorious twenty-fifth of October.

Companies E, I and K, led by Captain Kingsbury, under the direction of Major Hunt and Captain Hinton, staff-officers of Generals Curtis and Blunt, opened the ball at the Trading Post at four a. m., of October the twenty-fifth, by driving in the enemy's picket. It was this early movement that saved Fort Scott, for had not the advance of the first Division thus driven in the enemy's rear guard the battle would not have been opened by General Sanborn for two hours later and the enemy would have reached Fort Scott.

The same gallant squadrons were fore most in the charge upon the enemy's guns in the bottom beyond the Trading Post, the second of a series of fights that marked that day on the Marias des Cygnes and Osage. They participated in the brilliant cavalry charge at Mine Creek, which resulted in the capture of Marmaduke, Cabell, seven guns and a large body of prisoners. At Newtonia the Second Colorado, under Major Pritchard, with the Sixteenth Kansas, under Major Ketner, were first in the fight. In that battle, so brilliantly audacious, they largely contributed to the splendid result.

Forming a part of the nine hundred, who faced ten times their number, they stubbornly flung themselves against the foe, and for hours stood like a rock unyielding against the storm of bullets and the hurling tide of battle which fiercely dashed against our meagre lines, until the arrival of General Sanborn made certain the victory which had already gleamed about us. All honour to the gallant Colorado Volunteers, say we. We welcome them to our city, scarred and battle-worn heroes, as they are, and are only too proud to, in the same slight manner, acknowledge the great service we owe them.

There is very much, no doubt, that could have been told of the different encounters between the Second and the enemy, but as it was impossible to follow in their circuitous track at all times, I have endeavoured to make this history as interesting as I could with such information as I could gain from time to time in my travels, therewith trusting it will give pleasure to anyone who may deem it worth perusal.

More especially so to any Colorado soldier or their offspring. I will here add the rosters of the different companies as it may be interesting to the readers at some time or in some place, bringing to mind the name of a comrade when perhaps forgotten.

Appendix 2

LIST OF OFFICERS OF THE REGIMENT.
Field and Staff.

Colonel—
    James H. Ford.
Lieutenant-Colonel—
    Theo. H. Dodd.
First Major—
    S. S. Curtis.
Second Major—
    J. N. Smith.
Third Major—
    J. L. Pritchard.
Surgeon—
    I. J. Pollok.
Assistant Surgeons—
    Geo. S. Aiken,
    D. M. Vance.
Adjutant—
    R. S. Roe.
Quartermaster—
    G. C. Manville.
Commissary—
    James Burrell.
Chaplain—
    L. Hamilton.
Captains—
    Co. B—J. C. W. Hall,
    " E—W. H. Green,
    " F—George West,
    " G—E. D. Boyd,

Captains—
    Co. I—E. W. Kingsbury,
    " K—E. P. Elmer,
    " L—G. G. Norton,
    " M—Thomas Moses,
    " H—Charles Holly,
    " C—Cyrus DeForest,
    " A—I. F. Evans,
    " D—E. L. Berthuod.
First Lieutenants—
    Co. C—J. F. Seymour,
    " G—F. A. Spencer,
    " D—William Wise,
    " H—J. F. Bennet,
    " I—R. W. Jenkins,
    " L—U. B. Holloway,
    " K—George F. Crocker,
    " M—Wm. H. Pierce,
    " A—A. G. Clark,
    " F—W. H. Keith,
    " B—Jas. Parsons,
    " E—R. O. Rizer.
Second Lieutenants—
    Co. F—G. M. Richardson,
    " G—J. E. Tappan,
    " K—I. J. Stanton,
    " L—J. Cleaveland,
    " M—G. C. Bowen,
    " B—H. D. Jaynes,
    " H—A. L. Gooding,
    " C—M. Hennion,
    " I—C. A. Allen,
    " E—G. W. Culver,
    " D—F. M. Gravitt,
    " A—P. A. Ducey.

Roster of Company "A."

Captain—
  Isaac F. Evans.
First Lieutenant—
  Albert G. Clark,
Second Lieutenant—
  Patrick A. Ducey.
First Sergeant—
  Evan Jones.
Quartermaster Sergeant—
  George W. Howard.
Commissary Sergeant—
  Alex H. Reed.
Sergeants—
  William Cook,
  Jacob Sinex,
  Alex M. Staley,
  John Bay.
Corporals—
  Steven H. Warner,
  James Bremner,
  S. S. Kempton,
  Geo. W. Hardwick,
  John M. Gavran.
Buglers—
  Charles Williams,
  J. W. Shiffler.
Farrier—
  Luther C. Britton.
Blacksmith—
  John C. Dewitt.
Saddler—
  Joseph K. Fedrick.
Privates—
  William A. Aurner.
  Fayett Alferd,
  Joshua Armstrong,

Privates—
  Francis H. Bengley,
  Levi Benedict,
  John Burns,
  Wilson P. Burgasen,
  Charles Bernard,
  William Cox,
  Augustus R. Cox,
  Benjamin F. Carter,
  Lewis Chesser,
  Thomas Carroll,
  Thomas Connelly,
  John Dwyre,
  Willis Ellis,
  Lewis Ellis,
  Bartlet N. Fox,
  John Freel,
  William Gibbs,
  David Gharky,
  Benjamin Graham,
  Joseph Gerish,
  Henry Gillapp,
  Thomas Hodges,
  Chislian Herbacker,
  William Hayes,
  William C. Hadleigh,
  John H. Haskins,
  John Hall,
  Adolphus Ingham,
  John Kerrins,
  Thomas Kollar,
  John Kaineron,
  Ezra Lamb,
  Robert V. Lauder,
  Daniel Maher,
  Nelson McNeil,
  Alexander Maxwell,
  Thomas McFadden,
  Lindsay Mullinex,
  Patrick McGinnis,
  Bartholemew McDonough
  William Murphy,
  Andrew Ohler,
  John O'Brien,
  John Pillow,

Privates—
George W. Prosser,
Thomas Ramsay,
Michael J. Rogers,
William H. Rosson,
John Rosson.
Alfred G. Romine,
William W. Sugg,
David A. Stevens,
Abraham Shidler,
Thomas J. Sherod,
William H. Shaw,

Privates—
John C. Scott,
William S. Trow,
Dennis Tierney,
Joshua Taylor,
James F. Ulm,
Thomas J. Walls,
John Worrald,
George W. Wicks,
Peter Wells,
George L. Yant,
John K. Zoutsler.

Roster of Company "B."

Captain—
J. C. W. Hall,

First Lieutenant—
James Parsons.

Second Lieutenant—
Henry D. Jaynes.

First Sergeant—
William F. Kenton.

Quartermaster Sergeant—
Sydenham Mills.

Commissary Sergeant—
Andrew H. Grover.

Sergeants—
William H. Anderson,
Nathan H. Hopkins,
Martin D. Prentiss,
William Glasgow,
Garrett Feinan.

Corporals—
Edwin H. Sanford,
William W. Hodges,
Samuel Westerfield,
Joseph Mackrell,
Edwin P. Robinson,
Archibald Cribbs,

Corporals—
Uriah Simpson,
Michael Beacom.

Privates—
Horatio Allen,
Thomas Anderson,
Chauncey W. Amey,
John W. Ames,
Charles Arnold,
Comadore S. Brown,
Alexander Brown,
Harrison Berry,
John Branch,
Thomas Briggs,
Marcus T. Basset,
Alden G. Cate,
William H. Conklin,
James H. Custard,
Elisha Dewes,
Josiah M. Day,
Abram R. Daman,
William Emihizer,
Sylvester Gilson,
Simeon Haynes,
Charles Hitchburn,
Hiram Hawkins,
Alonzo F. Ickis,
William W. Johnson,
Justis B. Lloyd,
James H. Lykins,

Privates—
Ezra J. Lee,
Josiah P. Lesher,
Curtis Moore,
Simon Motz,
John Morrison,
Hugh Marshall,
Samuel Pickler,
Thomas Payne,
Josiah Porter,
Ludlo H. Pruden,
George Simpson,
Joseph M. W. Smith,
Amos N. Sylvester,
David Speilman.
Andrew Thomson,
John G. Thompson,
Harvey W. Thomas,
Joseph J. Thomas,
Seymour S. Vaughn,
George Williams,
James B. Wasson,
Jerome B. Wright,
John M. Weaver,

Privates—
William D. Withington,
Robert D. Alexander,
Robert Badley,
John C. Bowen,
George Bryan,
Lafayette Cofman,
George A. Cook,
William Carley,
Samuel Gastland,
William Emans,
Henry Estes,
William Fulbright,
Giles Gadard,
James A. Holmes,
Jacob Martin,
Henry Mateson,
Benjamin F. Nicholas,
Abijah H. Norris,
Charles L. Richardson,
James K. Scott,
Evan P. Shrivel,
Joseph Wizer,
William H. Wilson.

Roster of Company "C."

Captain—
Cyrus H. DeForest.

First Lieutenant—
J. Fenton Seymour.

Second Lieutenant—
Martin Hennion.

First Sergeant—
James M. Grover.

Quartermaster Sergeant—
Charles W. Burdsal.

Commissary Sergeant—
William Ogden.

Sergeants—
Samuel Peppard,
Delos. W. Babcock,

Sergeants—
Charles E. Holder,
Benjamin F. Chesrown.

Corporals—
Thomas Nolan,
Charles N. Sherman,
Charles H. Zuther,
James E. McNaughton,
Cyrus L. Hughes,
James B. Gardiner.

Blacksmith—
Thomas E. Ragsdale.

Saddler—
Daniel McDonnald.

Privates—
George Ashworth,
Thomas Brown,

Privates—
  Noah F. Brown,
  Edward Bard,
  John Brooks,
  James A. Caldwell,
  James T. Cully,
  William Chase,
  And. Clark,
  Francis Cooper,
  Bernard C. Click,
  William Dilley,
  Dennis M. Dickenow,
  Oliver E. Dalton,
  James. H. Dagner,
  Silas N. Dutton,
  Richard W. Evans,
  Henry A. Evans,
  William Fredericks,
  Le Grande Gould,
  Daniel M. Goodley,
  William A. Hunter,
  James A. Humphrey,
  Alfred N. Henry,
  Thomas C. Haller,
  William Howard,
  George W. Hill,
  Andrew L. Ingerson,
  Edward Johnson,
  Joseph Kenestrick,
  John C. Kelly,
  David La Belle,
  Napoleon La Belle,

Privates-
  Abel Lumbert,
  Allen P. Leggitt,
  John W. Long,
  Thomas McDermott,
  John S. Mount,
  John W. Mattock,
  John McNight,
  William B. Ogg,
  John Oberon,
  George Putnam,
  Theophilos C. Power,
  Joseph Richardson,
  Charles Robinson,
  James B. Rice,
  William P. Records,
  Daniel Sullivan,
  Albert H. Smart,
  Gordon C. Smart,
  William Smith,
  John Smith,
  Edward Tracey,
  William Terney,
  Ulysses E. Thurmond,
  James W. Thomas,
  John A. Wagner,
  James R. White,
  William Wolf,
  Tabor Wilcox,
  Jacob A. Woodmancy,
  Daniel J. Zent.

Roster of Company "D."

Captain—
  Edward L. Berthand.

First Lieutenant—
  William Wise.

Second Lieutenant—
  Francis M. Gravit.

First Sergeant—
  Anton Freeze.

Quartermaster Sergeant—
  William G. Pell.

Commissary Sergeant—
  Henry H. Lyon.

Sergeants—
  William J. Phillips,
  Henry J. Tibbitts,
  Morgan Knight,
  John T. Phillips.

Corporals—
    Walter H. Shade,
    William H. Lutshaw,
    Francis M. Gordon,
    Henry Ernst,
    William C. Teas,
    Alvin S. Carpenter,
    Michael B. Greaff.

Buglers—
    George W. Hobbs,
    James Garrison.

Clerk—
    John C. Northrup.

Farrier—
    William Garlach.

Blacksmith—
    Jackson Newkirk.

Saddler—
    James Douglass.

Privates—
    Joseph P. Abert,
    Philip Achey,
    Isaac W. Bailey,
    William H. Butch,
    George S. Bronson,
    Josiah Bacher,
    Nathaniel Brooks,
    Talbot J. Bullock,
    Eben Baird,
    John W. Bowen,
    Thomas Crider,
    George M. Chase,
    Thomas Conley.
    George B. Cooley,
    Horace C. Cartwright,
    Algernon S. Dutton,
    George M. Douglass,
    Abel F. Douglass,
    Charles Elder,
    David M. Emery,
    William H. Easly,
    William Irwin,
    Abraham Foust,
    Albert O. Griggs,
    John Geil,

Privates—
    Aaron Humphrey,
    John C. Hicks,
    James W. Hicks,
    Aquila Hicks,
    John Hotchkiss,
    Cyrus Hiltibidle,
    Charles Hedinger,
    Charles R. Jones,
    Alva A. Keeler,
    Irvin Knowlton,
    Christian Lange,
    Alphonse H. Lawrence,
    Otto Lamprecht,
    William H. Mathews,
    Patrick H. Mills,
    Thomas Morton,
    John Morris,
    David McIntosh,
    Wm. M. McConnell,
    Robert McCorkill,
    Isaiah McDowell,
    James McIsaacs,
    Morton O. Marvin,
    Nathaniel E. Nobles,
    Andrew J. Phillips,
    Robert Pointer,
    Leonard H. Randall,
    George W. Ross,
    Homer E. Ramsbury,
    Enos Southwick,
    Anson B. Southwick,
    Andrew M. Smith,
    Alfred P. Smith,
    Samuel Siloy,
    William H. Snider,
    Charles M. Sprague,
    James R. Spencer,
    Isaac D. Sibley,
    David Shanks,
    Lewis Trimble,
    Charles C. Toomer,
    Thomas F. Weaver,
    Lewis A. Waif,
    Jasper M. Wagner,
    Andrew J. West,
    Isaiah A. White,
    Frank C. Wright.

Roster of Company "E."

Captain—
  W. H. Green.

First Lieutenant—
  Robert O. Rizer.

Second Lieutenant—
  George W. Culver.

First Sergeant—
  Ezra Hoag.

Quartermaster Sergeant—
  John R. Adams.

Commissary Sergeant—
  John L. Keutner.

Sergeants—
  Wm. Lockstone,
  David C. Nettleton,
  Wm. P. Shockley,
  Henry Clark,
  Henry Coy.

Corporals—
  Oliver Howard
  James Fulsom,
  Philip Hayes,
  Charles Pickard,
  William G. Dunn.

Saddler
  Lewis Hoffman.

Buglers—
  Henry Neymeyer,
  Thomas Willey.

Farrier—
  Isaac Hannah.

Privates—
  Elisha Andrews,
  William H. Ashton,
  Thomas Asquith,
  William Brown,

Privates—
  John Baker,
  Horatio Banning,
  Charles W. Chealey,
  Stephen Culbertson,
  Stephen Conroy,
  Daniel M. Clark,
  Joseph Creely,
  Aureu L. Crane,
  John Cain,
  William Cummins,
  Oscar F. Eddy,
  John E. Finney,
  Eugene Flint,
  Joseph P. Gard,
  A. L. Glen,
  Julius Garranflo,
  Thomas Gray,
  Lyman Graves,
  Marshall T. Hayward,
  Thomas Harrington,
  Mathias D. Huston,
  Charles H. Hannam,
  John Hegitswheler,
  John H. G. Holmes,
  George F. Havens,
  Daniel V. Hubbard,
  Luther C. Horr,
  Jonathan Ingram,
  James Iker,
  John Jennings,
  James T. Kelso,
  John Kessinger,
  Edward Kyle,
  Frank Lusher,
  Justus Leslie,
  Henry Leis,
  James H. Morrison,
  Patrick McDonough,
  Daniel McCleery,
  John McDonald,
  Jacob L. Nickam,
  John W. Olingemach,
  Robert Riley,
  Norman Reynolds,

Privates—
Peter Robertson,
Geo. W. Richardson,
James B. Ross,
John Stone,
George Spencer,
Benjamin F. Sherod,
Samuel E. Smith,
William Simpson,
John Simpson,
John M. Shore,
F. J. Smith,
Walter B. Tillotson,
John Walker,

Privates—
William Walker,
Charles B. Withrow,
George Wett,
John W. Bailey,
Israel Eaton.
John S. Graham,
Stephen Higley,
George A. Putnam,
Palmer Tiffany,
Charles Turner.

Regimental Armorer—
Wm. Weisner.

Roster of Company "F."

Captain—
George West.
First Lieutenant—
M. H. Keith.
Second Lieutenant—
George H. Richardson.
First Sergeant—
N. B. McMannaman.
Quartermaster Sergeant—
William B. Gillispie.
Commissary Sergeant—
Luther K. Crane.
Sergeants—
Moses S. Strew,
Benjamin E. Gump,
Robert S. West,
John Saet,
William W. Babbit.
Corporals—
John M. Collier,
William Neeley,
William Kimbal,
Martin V. Wilder,

Corporals—
Oliver D. Holliday,
Levi S. McGrew,
Abbott W. Sanderson,
William Gorgas.
Buglers—
John C. Barteolett,
John F. McCleery.
Farrier—
Thomas Hunter.
Blacksmith—
C. B. Reynolds.
Saddler—
William S. Flanegan.
Privates—
Roderick Allen,
John Aull,
James Beasley,
Philip Beemer,
Joseph Bennett,
Charles Baker,
Theo. B. Berch,
Robert P. Bobst,
Morton Bristol,
George Brundy,

Privates—
  Joseph Bosley,
  Alexander Campbell,
  Richard Cheney,
  Amos Darraw,
  Andrew H. Dennis,
  Isaac W. Denton,
  George Elliott,
  Charles Elgen,
  Joseph S. Feilds,
  Thomas Flemming,
  Frank Ferrell,
  Ernest Carl Frank,
  John E. Greene,
  John Groce,
  William Hart,
  Alexander Hamilton,
  John B. Huggins,
  James R. Hunter,
  Elijah Hurst,
  Jacob Jarrett,
  Daniel Keely,
  John Kieef,
  Joseph M. Kelly,
  William Kinner,
  William H. Kimble,
  William H. Latham,

Privates—
  Charles Lochman,
  James I. Martin,
  William Marshall,
  John McCardle,
  John H. Mahler,
  Arthur McClure,
  George McCrillis,
  William McMakin,
  Daniel Muffitt,
  William Nichols,
  Henry L. Neimon.
  George O'Brian,
  William H. Pruett,
  William Patterson,
  Edward Riley,
  Andrew J. Stacy,
  Adna Stephens,
  James Smith,
  Silas P. Sutton,
  Henry A. Tortat,
  John Teeter,
  John Tummons,
  Stagg C. Thompson,
  Hans Wulff,
  Edward L. Young,
  Felders M. Young.

Roster of Company "G."

Captain—
  E. D. Boyd.
First Lieutenant—
  Fred. A. Spencer.
Second Lieutenant—
  John S. Tappan.
First Sergeant—
  Enos R. Lee.
Quartermaster Sergeant—
  Aylmer Keith.
Commissary Sergeant—
  Charles M. Lewis.

Sergeants—
  William B. Hawk,
  George W. Lane,
  Patrick McCristal.
  Chapin S. Fay,
  James G. Mygatt.

Corporals—
  Joseph A. Shaw,
  John A. Mulholland,
  David H. Bradford,
  David La Rue,
  Dennis S. Langton,
  John Lent,
  George G. Selleg.

Farrier—
  John D. James.

Saddler—
  Thomas Gleason.

Buglers—
  Benjamin F. Spillars,
  Owen O. Johnston.

Privates—
  Henry M. Arnold,
  Henry F. Atherton,
  Walter Atkins,
  Francis M. Brownfield,
  Dwight A. Ball,
  John Boyer,
  Andrew Bradford,
  John Braithwaite,
  Joseph M. Butcher,
  Molden Bledsoe,
  Jefferson Campbell,
  Stewart Campbell,
  Alva Chamberlaine,
  John Chittick,
  Joseph Cody,
  William S. Conner,
  Frederick Davis,
  James T. Donohoe,
  Patrick H. Donohoe,
  Charles Dougherty,
  Morton W. Elsworth,
  August Engleman,
  David Fowler,
  Chester F. Fowler.
  John Freestone,
  Harry Galbransen,
  John Grazier,

Privates—
  Jesse Hendricks,
  Cornelius M. Johnson,
  Edward A. Jones,
  James Keen,
  John La Belle,
  John Lacy,
  Elyeer S. I. La Fountaine,
  Samuel H. Lemmon,
  Henry Livingston,
  John Loughry,
  Alexander E. Love,
  James McDowell,
  James H. McVay,
  Moses Miles,
  James A. Mitchel,
  William T. Morehead,
  Henry E. Oates,
  James Orton,
  George W. Perkins,
  Alfred Pyzer,
  Edward Rhoades.
  Luther A. Rogers,
  Jesse Riley,
  John Rottmaster,
  Marquis D. Salisbury,
  Wm. H. Self,
  Wm. Smith,
  Charles Sovereign,
  William Spencer,
  David Stewart,
  Mortimer Stone,
  Caleb G. Thorp,
  Peter Vandermade,
  Jefferson Waltea,
  William White,
  William Williams,
  John D. Young.

Roster of Company "H."

Captain—
  Charles F. Holly.

First Lieutenant—
  James F. Bennett.

Second Lieutenant—
  Albert L. Gooding.

First Sergeant—
  B. F. Johnston.

Quartermaster Sergeant—
    Augustus Frederick.
Commissary Sergeant—
    Edward P. Davis.
Sergeants—
    George H. Goodwin,
    John M. Moore,
    Thomas Hooper,
    Ebenezer Jones,
    Daniel R. Wagstaff.
Corporals—
    Samuel P. Hatter,
    Andrew B. Budd,
    Clark C. Martin,
    C. A. Schilowsky,
    Hiram C. Olmstead,
    Joseph Colt,
    Levi Hill,
    John Pendroy.
Buglers—
    John W. Torrence,
    Levi Allen.
Saddler—
    Eugene B. Palmer.
Farrier—
    Jordon Scott.
Blacksmith—
    Joseph Kuhn,
Clerk—
    C. L. Moore.
Privates—
    George Ammel,
    William H. Allen,
    John Bair,
    William Bentley,
    William S. Buckwalter,
    John N. Bond,
    Fernando L. Bradley,
    Henry S. Bank,
    Benjamin B. Bates,
    John H. Coleman,

Privates—
    John Carrothers,
    Dyer A. Conklin,
    Bartholomew Cole,
    Samuel D. Cowdez,
    Thomas Carlson,
    Robert E. Constant,
    James L. Craft,
    Joel W. Disbrow,
    Francis A. Drullard,
    Noah H. Eaves,
    John W. Foot,
    Rensaler Falkner,
    Friend S. Gale,
    Alexander Hamilton,
    William H. Hewitt,
    Benton S. Harbeur,
    Levi L. Hughes,
    William H. Hopkins,
    Francis G. Havens,
    William W. Jones,
    Charles Jirman,
    John Johnstone,
    Edward F. Kingland,
    John W. Kelso,
    Edwin R. Knight,
    Albert Koenig,
    James Karr,
    Orlean H. Lomiss,
    Henry F. Lentz,
    Stephen B. Layburn,
    Edward Metcalf,
    William McBride,
    Michael McKinney,
    Alexander McMasters,
    Thomas D. McLain,
    David S. Miller,
    Jesse H. Northrup,
    William W. Northrup,
    William F. Newkirk,
    Elisha P. Plummer,
    James W. Purdy,
    Richard H. Quin,
    Christian W. Ries,
    James Ragen,
    Benjamin F. Rafferty,
    Henry Steiner,
    David B. Sweep,

Privates—
  John E. Sawyer,
  John J. Shultz,
  Henry Schoepile,
  John Sykes,
  William E. Stubbs,
  William Tomkins,

Privates—
  Orville Talbott,
  Jacob H. Valentine,
  Oliver V. Wallace,
  Elisha T. Weaver,
  Luther C. Woodward.

Roster of Company "I."

Captain—
  Ezra W. Kingsbury.

First Lieutenant—
  Richard W. Jenkins.

Second Lieutenant—
  Charles A. Allen.

First Sergeant—
  Samuel S. Ferree.

Quartermaster Sergeant—
  Charles C. True.

Commissary Sergeant—
  Edward S. Hoole.

Sergeants—
  Theophilus Taylor,
  Walter Bown,
  Charles G. Lawrence,
  Miles Jain.

Corporals—
  George Croak,
  Nathaniel G. Plummer,
  Uri L. Peck,
  Freeman Belcher,
  Hamilton C. Martin,
  Joseph N. Steward,
  Joshua H. Cook,
  Royal P. Haven.

Buglers—
  Godfrey Ulrich,
  Walter H. Wilson.

Blacksmith—
  Thoma Mohan.

Privates—
  Jacob Bard,
  Robert Barr,
  Andrew Branson,
  Sylvanus Budd,
  William Beck,
  Lafayette Bailey,
  Milo Brewster,
  John Barnes,
  Adolph Black,
  William H. Cook,
  David W. Critzer,
  William W. Colburne,
  Palmer K. A. Chaffee,
  Marcus Cooper,
  Silas Clark,
  Lester S. Case,
  John M. Coleman,
  James H. Coulter,
  Oscar M. Cady,
  John Donaldson,
  Thomas Dunn,
  Martin P. Daily,
  Royal Denison,
  Charles Emmons,
  John Evans,
  James M. Eaman,
  William H. Fee,
  David C. Frame,
  James M. Frame,
  Daniel Gift,
  William D. Gross,
  John S. Granger,

Privates—
    George Golden,
    George F. Greenup,
    Alexander Harvell,
    Charles F. Heycus,
    William H. Heycus,
    Samuel Holbrook,
    Charles Hathaway,
    Jacob S. Kehler,
    John King,
    John Kensler,
    Samuel Knox,
    David A. Lykins,
    Charles H. Lewis,
    William A. Lawrence,
    Enos McLaughlin,
    Andrew Moore,
    Robert W. Moffitt,
    Andrew Munsch,
    Joseph Oumer,

Privates—
    Anson W. Peters,
    George Palsgraf,
    Daniel Preffer,
    Rufus Rice,
    Aaron Runyan,
    James F. Rowe,
    Patrick Sullivan,
    George Shirley,
    John W. Taffee,
    Thomas Taylor,
    Elliott C. Tuttle,
    William Templeton,
    John W. Vaughan,
    Jame Wood,
    Henry Whitmore,
    Cornelius W. Wright,
    Thomas Webb,
    Thomas M. Walker.

Roster of Company "K."

Captain—
    E. P. Elmer.

First Lieutenant—
    George F. Crocker.

Second Lieutenant—
    B. F. Johnson.

Quartermaster Sergeant—
    James T. Clark.

Commissary Sergeant—
    Austin H. Weir.

Sergeants—
    Jeremiah H. Coney
    Jesse Knight,
    James H. Stocker.

Corporals—
    John S. Harper,
    Lewis Coleman,
    Joseph N. Dodsor,

Corporals—
    Andrew A. Burk,
    John M. Wilkerson,
    William A. Fortune,
    Charles Edwards,
    Henry H. Lacy.

Farrier—
    Henderson Roy.

Saddler—
    William J. Barnes.

Bugler—
    William H. Carroll.

Privates—
    George W. Black,
    Squire B. Bosworth,
    Adoniram J. Bowen.
    Samuel P. Butler,
    James Campbell,
    Wilson Cooley,
    Peter Cummings,

Privates—
William H. Derickson,
George W. Dickerson,
Charles W. Dorwin,
James M. Duncan,
John H. Fortune,
Charles W. Gorsuch,
Refus H. Heath,
Horatio F. Heald,
Peter Heintz,
William H. Houck,
Samuel J. Huestis,
Alexander Hughes,
Charles H. Hughes,
James B. Hayles,
William H. Hogan,
Joseph Hays,
George M. Hicks,
Monroe James,
Laurens H. Johnston,
Williams C. Kellogg,
Albert O. Locke,
John A. Lowe,
Thomas B. Lane,
James Loak,
Levi McLaughlin,
Peter J. McMartin,
Gerhard Mermann,

Privates—
Seth R. Mills,
Thomas B. Morton,
Joseph Maier,
Hans Mundt,
William McConnor,
Rody McSorley,
Horace H. Norton,
Horace Norton,
Aaron Nyswanger,
Asa F. Powers,
Morris Peck,
Michael H. Reece,
John F. Rigney,
Alonzo G. Russell,
Milford H. Sanders,
Erastus B. Smith,
Stephen Slaughter,
John Straley,
Joseph H. Sanborn,
Thomas Tracey,
William Tabor,
John A. Washburn,
Joseph Wells,
Joseph Wetherill,
Thomas B. Williams,
John Williams,
Walter Weston.

Roster of Company "L."

Captain—
Uriah B. Holloway.

First Lieutenant—
Irving W. Stanton.

Second Lieutenant—
James S. Cleveland.

First Sergeant—
Carmi B. Vaughn.

Quartermaster Sergeant—
Alfred A. Waggoner.

Commissary Sergeant—
Christopher S. Philipps.

Sergeants—
John B. Rupe,
Henry Brown,
Samuel W. Fitzgerald,
Norman Parker,
Montgomery Wisner.

Corporals—
Allen J. Davis,
Robert H. Dunlap,
William K. Anthony,
William H. Hardy,
John Bremner,
Rufus B. Edwards,
Egbert E. Wills,
Charles Thorow.

Buglers—
  George W. Albright,
  Daniel Welshons.
Farrier—
  Nathaniel Simpson.
Blacksmith—
  James M. Blam.
Saddler—
  Willard B. Austin.
Armorer—
  Peter Duffey.
Privates—
  Robert W. Adams,
  John Wesley Brown,
  John F. Blair,
  Rodney C. Bean,
  Joachim Borchert,
  Cyrus G. Byers,
  Lemuel N. Bradley,
  Philip Bromler,
  Archibald Bennett,
  Henry Bartlett,
  Cary D. Chapman,
  John Carpenter,
  Lewis Dufrain,
  James Doyle,
  George W. Davidson,
  Henry H. French,
  John Fletcher,
  John Grubb,
  Dudley W. Griswold,
  Abednego Gilmore,

Privates—
  John C Gilispie,
  John Glidewell,
  Frederick G. Her,
  James Johnstone,
  James Kelsay,
  John Kraft,
  Charles H. Miller,
  Mathew McCune,
  Sullivan McKibbon,
  Zebulon B. More,
  Jerry McLaughlin,
  Henry Neighbours,
  Wallace Pumphrey,
  William G. Root,
  Charles Root,
  Rafalo Romero,
  Leonard Sergeant,
  William Sage,
  William J. Spencer,
  Isaac M. Scearce,
  Charles E. Sullivan,
  William H. Stone,
  Columbus Tuttle,
  George Tuttle,
  Myron Tuttle,
  Nathan M. Turk,
  Joshua Vickroy,
  Samuel S. Wills,
  William Welsnhons,
  Thomas Ward,
  Charles M. Webster,
  Oliver Wooley,
  Joseph Allen,
  John Warren Brown.

Roster of Company "M."

Captain—
  Thomas Moses.
First Lieutenant—
  William Pierce.
Second Lieutenant—
  George C. Bowan.

First Sergeant—
  Daniel G. W. Whiting,
Quartermaster Sergeant—
  William J. Lawrence.
Commissary Sergeant—
  J. Fitz. James Cooper.

Sergeants—
  Charles Leslie,
  Joseph Baker,
  Isaac S. Freeman,
  James C. Whitall,
  John H. Sowell.

Corporals—
  Ferdinand Sigel,
  George M. McDougall,
  William Linsdale,
  Daniel T. Mack,
  Merritt C. Foster,
  William H. Garlic,
  Austin W. Means,
  John W. Peterson.

Buglers—
  John T. Sheppard,
  William Stewart.

Farriers—
  Henry Seiffert.
  George E Dorman,

Saddler—
  William H. Robbins,

Privates—
  William Clark,
  Charles Cole,
  Joseph F. Cole,
  Clayton S. Donihue,
  William J. Doneley
  Henry Day,
  William F. Earl,
  Jaques Fredez,
  John Fidler,
  John P. Frederic,
  Christopher C. Fergeson,
  William P. Fox,
  William W. Frame,
  August Grenneman,
  William H. Griffith,

Privates—
  Francis Goodwin,
  Christopher L. Hess,
  William Hoen,
  William E. Hill,
  John Harress,
  Diego Hernandez,
  Charles A. Henry,
  Joseph Houghtaling,
  Joseph Johnson,
  James Johnson,
  Albert Kizer,
  John C. Kanditer,
  George W. Lewis,
  Henry N. Lewis,
  James J. Ladd,
  William Laughlin,
  William H. H. Lowe,
  William Mavis,
  William Murray,
  Asbury McKnight,
  William McDougal,
  David F. Needham,
  Joab B. North,
  John A. Owens,
  Garrett Perrine,
  Nehemiah R. Packard,
  Andrew P. Phenning,
  Henry W. Pulver,
  John Quin,
  Louis Reynolds,
  Benford Smith,
  Isaiah B. Smith,
  Jackson D. Slaughter,
  Jesse C. Strickland,
  Henry C. Scoville,
  William Sanders,
  John Thompson,
  Henry A. Tage,
  Alec Wray,
  Lewis M. Watson,
  Robert Wilkinson.

TABLE OF STATISTICS.

Alphabetical List of Trades and Nationalities in the Regiment.

Trade	Count	Trade	Count
Accountants	2	Laborers	73
Actors	3	Masons	9
Artists	3	Merchants	9
Ambrotypist	1	Machinists	4
Apothecary	1	Music Teacher	1
Brewer	1	Millers	9
Butchers	9	Moulders	3
Brick-makers	2	Millwrights	9
Bakers	7	Mechanics	15
Barber	1	Musicians	8
Boatmen	11	Miners	462
Book-keeper	1	Newsdealer	1
Blacksmiths	25	Physicians	6
Builder	1	Pilots	2
Cabinet-maker	1	Printers	17
Carpenters	35	Plumber	1
Cooks	3	Plasterers	7
Contractor	1	Ranch men	7
Clerks	16	Silversmith	1
Collier	1	Stone Cutters	3
Coopers	6	Stone Masons	5
Drummers	3	Salesmen	2
Druggists	5	Sailors	9
Drover	1	Ship Carpenter	1
Dentists	2	Shoe-makers	14
Dancing Master	1	Soldiers	8
Engineers	15	Servant	1
Engravers	2	Stage Drivers	3
Florists	2	Tinker	1
Freighters	2	Traders	2
Farmers	235	Turners	5
Glove-maker	1	Tailors	4
Gunsmiths	10	Teamsters	35
Hostler	1	Upholsterers	3
Harness-makers	2	Veterinary Surgeon	1
Hunters	2	Wagon-makers	2
Joiners	4	Watch-maker	1
Locksmith	1	Waggoner	1
Lawyers	9		

NATIONALITIES.

United States.

Maine	32
New Hampshire	10
Vermont	81
Massachusetts	26
Rhode Island	4
Connecticut	17
New York	163
New Jersey	17
Pennsylvania	110
Delaware	2
Maryland	10
Virginia	23
North Carolina	4
South Carolina	2
Alabama	2
Ohio	202
Kentucky	38
Missouri	46
Indiana	31
Illinois	65
Michigan	16
Iowa	15
Wisconsin	6
Minnesota	1
Tennessee	19

Other Countries.

New Mexico	22
Cherokee Nation	1
Choctaw Nation	1
Canada	32
England	36
Ireland	63
Scotland	15
Wales	2
Australia	1
Prussia	7
Germany	42
Poland	4
Denmark	1
Sweden	5
Russia	1
Norway	4
France	7
Bohemia	1
Saxony	2
Holland	2
Bavaria	1
Switzerland	1
Born at Sea	3
Nationality Unknown	1

ALSO FROM LEONAUR
AVAILABLE IN SOFTCOVER OR HARDCOVER WITH DUST JACKET

THE WOMAN IN BATTLE by Loreta Janeta Velazquez—Soldier, Spy and Secret Service Agent for the Confederacy During the American Civil War.

BOOTS AND SADDLES by Elizabeth B. Custer—The experiences of General Custer's Wife on the Western Plains.

FANNIE BEERS' CIVIL WAR by Fannie A. Beers—A Confederate Lady's Experiences of Nursing During the Campaigns & Battles of the American Civil War.

LADY SALE'S AFGHANISTAN by Florentia Sale—An Indomitable Victorian Lady's Account of the Retreat from Kabul During the First Afghan War.

THE TWO WARS OF MRS DUBERLY by Frances Isabella Duberly—An Intrepid Victorian Lady's Experience of the Crimea and Indian Mutiny.

THE REBELLIOUS DUCHESS by Paul F. S. Dermoncourt—The Adventures of the Duchess of Berri and Her Attempt to Overthrow French Monarchy.

NURSE EDITH CAVELL by William Thomson Hill & Jacqueline Van Til—Two accounts of a Notable British Nurse of the First World War. The Martyrdom of Nurse Cavell by William Thompson Hill, With Edith Cavell by Jacqueline Van Til

NURSE AND SPY IN THE UNION ARMY by Sarah Emma Evelyn Edmonds—During the American Civil War

WIFE NO. 19 by Ann Eliza Young—The Life & Ordeals of a Mormon Woman During the 19th Century

DIARY OF A NURSE IN SOUTH AFRICA by Alice Bron—With the Dutch-Belgian Red Cross During the Boer War

FIELD HOSPITAL AND FLYING COLUMN by Violetta Thurstan—With the Red Cross on the Western & Eastern Fronts During the First World War.

THE MEMSAHIB & THE MUTINY by R. M. Coopland—An English lady's ordeals in Gwalior and Agra during the Indian Mutiny 1857

MY CAPTIVITY AMONG THE SIOUX INDIANS by Fanny Kelly—The ordeal of a pioneer woman crossing the Western Plains in 1864

WITH MAXIMILIAN IN MEXICO by Sara Yorke Stevenson—A Lady's experience of the French Adventure

PERSONAL RECOLLECTIONS OF JOAN OF ARC by Mark Twain

AVAILABLE ONLINE AT **www.leonaur.com**
AND FROM ALL GOOD BOOK STORES

ALSO FROM LEONAUR
AVAILABLE IN SOFTCOVER OR HARDCOVER WITH DUST JACKET

A DIARY FROM DIXIE by Mary Boykin Chesnut—A Lady's Account of the Confederacy During the American Civil War

FOLLOWING THE DRUM by Teresa Griffin Vielé—A U. S. Infantry Officer's Wife on the Texas frontier in the Early 1850's

FOLLOWING THE GUIDON by Elizabeth B. Custer—The Experiences of General Custer's Wife with the U. S. 7th Cavalry.

LADIES OF LUCKNOW by G. Harris & Adelaide Case—The Experiences of Two British Women During the Indian Mutiny 1857. A Lady's Diary of the Siege of Lucknow by G. Harris, Day by Day at Lucknow by Adelaide Case

MARIE-LOUISE AND THE INVASION OF 1814 by Imbert de Saint-Amand—The Empress and the Fall of the First Empire

SAPPER DOROTHY by Dorothy Lawrence—The only English Woman Soldier in the Royal Engineers 51st Division, 79th Tunnelling Co. during the First World War

"TELL IT ALL" by Fanny Stenhouse—The Ordeals of a Woman Against Polygamy Within the Mormon Church During the 19th Century

FRIENDS AND FOES IN THE TRANSKEI by Helen M. Prichard—A Victorian lady's experience of Southern Africa during the 1870's

MEMOIRS OF SARAH DUCHESS OF MARLBOROUGH, AND OF THE COURT OF QUEEN ANNE VOLUMES 1 & 2 by A. T. Thomson

THE WHITE SLAVE MARKET by Mrs. Archibald Mackirdy (Olive Christian Malvery) and William Nicholas Willis—An Overview of the Traffic in Young Women at the Turn of the Nineteenth and Early Twentieth Centuries

MARY PORTER GAMEWELL AND THE SIEGE OF PEKING by A. H. Tuttle—An American Lady's Experiences of the Boxer Uprising, China 1900

VANISHING ARIZONA by Martha Summerhayes—A young wife of an officer of the U.S. 8th Infantry in Apacheria during the 1870's

THE RIFLEMAN'S WIFE by Mrs. Fitz Maurice—*The Experiences of an Officer's Wife and Chronicles of the Old 95th During the Napoleonic Wars*

THE OATMAN GIRLS by Royal B. Stratton—The Capture & Captivity of Two Young American Women in the 1850's by the Apache Indians

AVAILABLE ONLINE AT **www.leonaur.com**
AND FROM ALL GOOD BOOK STORES

www.ingramcontent.com/pod-product-compliance
Lightning Source LLC
Chambersburg PA
CBHW021009090426
42738CB00007B/715